Looking at World Religions

Series editor Roy Pitcher

Meeting Hinduism

W Owen Cole

Principal Lecturer and Head of Religious Studies at West Sussex Institute of Higher Education, Chichester

Longman

For Manu

Acknowledgements

The author would like to thank members of the Bharatiya Vidya Bhavan in India and Britain for their help and hospitality, and many other Hindu friends including Hemant Kanitkar who read the manuscript and made many useful suggestions.

Contents

1
Introduction

India is both a country and a continent. Its many states form the world's largest democracy, a republic with its own president as head of state, but also a member of the British Commonwealth.

The vastness of India is hard to describe. No one can imagine a population of 750 million people, or a surface area of over 1 200 000 square miles (3 250 000 square kilometres). To get some idea of the size of the country, imagine taking a rail journey from Bombay to Delhi. This is a distance of 1542 kilometres and takes the best part of two days. Leaving Bombay at 5.25 one morning you would be on the move continuously for the whole of that day and the next. At 9.20 pm you would reach your destination. If you decided to go on to Amritsar, that would take another eight hours or more. As you travelled from one region to another, the writing on the platform signs and advertisements seen from the carriage window would change from Gujerati to Hindi to Punjabi – all totally different scripts. Some of your fellow passengers might have come from south of Bombay and be speaking Tamil or Malayalam; a family returning to Amritsar would probably be speaking Punjabi; a couple journeying to New Delhi would be talking in Hindi; yet they might all be reading English language newspapers, magazines or novels. Sometimes English, which is taught in most secondary schools, is the only language which such a group of people share, though there is a move to encourage all Indians to become Hindi speakers. After all, Hindi is an Indian language, English is a foreign language brought to India by the British.

The climate in India is uniform in one respect, the summer temperature is very hot everywhere. In fact, Indians like to joke that they have only three seasons in their country: hot, very hot and warm. It is never cold except in mountainous areas and at night between November and February. In the northern plains it sometimes gets cold enough for frost, but not often.

PLANNED FAMILY
A HAPPY FAMILY

नियोजित परिवार सुख का आधार

▲

1 Hindi and English can be found in many parts of India, as at this bus stop in Delhi, but regional languages are also important. The campaign encouraging birth control has met with some success.

One of the most remarkable facts about India is that it is a flourishing democracy even though it only became independent in 1947, having been ruled by the Mughals who invaded India and occupied Delhi in 1526 CE (Common Era) and then by the British. For over four hundred years Indians had not been masters in their own home.

The majority of India's population – perhaps 650 million – are Hindus, but India is a secular democracy. This means that all the many religions are respected but none is given preference or privilege. The main festivals of all the religions may be kept as holidays by people who work in schools or government offices, but trains and buses run on those days, shops remain open and much of life goes on as usual. In fact, most people have to celebrate their festivals as best they can when they can, often in the evening or at night. In summer the evening or night is the only time when it is cool enough for adults to find the energy for festivities. Children seem to be lively no matter what the time of day.

Religion plays a part in the life of almost every Indian and almost every aspect of life is religious, certainly as far as Hindus are concerned. Even the early morning bathe, whether it be in a river or pond or under the shower in a house in one of the cities, is a religious act of purification, not just a means of refreshment.

What is Hinduism?

The religion of the vast majority of Indians is Hinduism. To define it very precisely is impossible. Many Hindus themselves might describe it as the religion of those Indians who are not Muslims, Sikhs, Christians, Parsees, Jains, Buddhists, Jews, or members of some other religion. It is the religion of the Indian people, and is as varied as the appearance and language of the people themselves.

The word Hinduism is not an Indian term. It was originally the name given by non-Indians to refer to the people who lived east of the river Indus. There was no need for the Indians to name their religion until foreigners asked them to describe it. When attempting such a description, Hindus will often use the phrase 'sanatana dharma'. Dharma is the nearest word Hindus have to the English 'religion', but it can also mean custom, tradition, or way of life. Sanatana dharma means something like 'the eternal way of life'. The rest of this book is an attempt to explain the phrase more fully. Hinduism is the world's oldest religion. It is also a universal religion, a way of life for everyone. Many Hindus consider Christianity and Islam, as well as Buddhism, Sikhism and Jainism which have their roots in the Indian religious tradition, as forms of Hinduism. They will also point out that it covers every aspect of life. Dharma is an all-embracing word.

TASKS TASKS TASKS TASKS TASKS TASKS

1 Mount a large map of India on the classroom wall. Note where the cities of Delhi, Madras, Calcutta, Bombay, Amritsar, Varanasi (Banares) and Mathura (on the river Jumna–Yamuna) are.
Collect colour photographs from travel brochures, find which places they depict on the map, mount them round the borders of the map, using string and pins to link them with their location on the map.
Find examples of Indian scripts. Paste them on to the map, being careful to attach them to the regions where you would expect to see them on public notices.

2 On your own blank map of India mark the following: Delhi, Bombay, Calcutta, the river Ganges, the river Jumna–Yamuna, Hardwar, Varanasi (Banares) and Mathura on the Jumna.

3 Try to assemble an exhibition of costume dolls, Hindu artefacts and Indian pictures showing the variety of Indian culture.

2
Hindu villages

Over eighty per cent of the inhabitants of India live in villages. If you fly over the country in an aeroplane, you will see them dotted across the landscape, separated from one another by the small, rectangular fields which fan out from them. It is in these fields that most villagers work day after day.

It is impossible to describe a typical Indian or Hindu village. The size and layout, even the materials used by the inhabitants for building their houses, vary greatly. The same is true of their economic and technological development. In the state of Punjab all the villages have electricity and most are connected to the big cities by tarmac roads. Many of the houses have their own piped water supply or at least their own hand pumps. Much remains to be done, but rough cart tracks, village wells and dependence upon oil lamps

▼
2 This village in north-eastern India is still focused on the pond; elsewhere it has often become unimportant.

and candles are becoming the exception rather than the rule. Each year another two or three thousand villages in India are being supplied with mains electricity. When this happens there will soon be someone who buys a television set and this brings the village into contact with the outside world in the form of New Delhi or a state capital. Otherwise there is always the transistor radio which can be heard in many homes. The touring cinema is very popular too. The projector is mounted on a lorry and powered by a diesel generator. A temporary screen is put up and everyone sits on the ground in the dark, warm evening. Travel is quite cheap, even by Indian standards, and this is a country where people seem to be constantly on the move. They begin at dawn or before and city streets are still busy at ten o'clock in the evening, four hours after darkness has fallen and the last shops have shut.

Rich villagers often live in houses built of kiln-baked bricks with sloping tiled roofs or flat cemented ones. Such houses are often called pukka. However, these are not always the best buildings to live in even though they are a status symbol. They become desperately hot in the summer and very cold in winter, especially if they have stone floors. More sensible are the houses commonly lived in by poorer folk. These have a thatched or wood and plaster roof, unburnt clay-brick walls and beaten earth floors. It is not too unusual to find well-off people moving for comfort into store houses built of these materials, when the heat makes their grand houses unbearable, even with the big cooling fans which hang from the ceilings spinning as fast as they can.

▲
3 Bihar is regarded as a poor region of India but this picture of a village in Bihar shows how dangerous it is to generalise.

▼
4 The sight of oxen providing power for the fodder-chopping machine seen in the foreground is less common today. Electric power is gradually taking over.

Village layouts

Although they could not be described as typical village layouts the following three examples have features common to many villages:

Ramdaspur

Our first example, let us call it Ramdaspur (near Varanasi), has about sixty houses in it. Its finest houses are close to the road. The biggest is owned by a rich man whose eldest son now lives in the USA. His two other sons run a business in Bombay. All three send money home regularly. That explains the existence of a large red-brick house, standing proudly above the other houses in the village, a television aerial protruding from its flat roof. The rich man is a brahmin, belonging to a group of people who traditionally acted as priests. Occasionally he performs such duties for the village but mainly he looks after his land and various village matters. The two other brahmin houses are nearby and similar to his, though not quite as big. One tube well is shared by the occupants of all three houses.

Walking along the path beyond these houses one comes to the village pond, now only a resting place for a few water birds, somewhere for the buffalo to cool off in the heat of the day, and where the children can splash about. Nearby fields are irrigated from it. Its water is no longer used for drinking and the clothes are washed beside the tube wells now. Beyond the pond stand the twenty houses of the goalas, the buffalo-owning families. They are all single storey. Some are semi-detached but most are in two lines of terraced housing. By looking carefully it is possible to see that one has been added to another over a period of time. As a family has grown in size it has added an extension. A few of the houses are of red burnt brick, the rest are the colour of the clay from which they have been made. Their walls are smooth and their roofs perfectly flat. They have only small windows which are mainly for ventilation and to let in some light. Except in the rainy season from July to September, life is lived mostly outdoors. A house is a place for storing things, hence the strong doors. Until the very cold nights come in late October or November, people even sleep outside – on light bedsteads called charpoys.

The buffalo are tethered; so that they will not trample the grain which is growing in the fields. Some of the boys and girls take them food – hay and green vegetable leaves from the fields. Older boys have gone into the town with some of the men to sell their milk in the market. The recently built tarmac road is what has brought the goalas their wealth. The old trackway which it replaced was so rough that all the milk would have spilled long before it reached the city; if any were left, it would have become sour before it had travelled the ten miles, a journey which would have taken at least four hours.

Further on, at the north end of the village is a large, rectangular, single-storey, stone building covered over with grey cement. This serves as a school, though lessons are usually outdoors; it is also used as a dispensary when a doctor and team of health workers make their occasional visits. At the northern fringe is a flat open area in front of two small temples, one to Hanuman, the monkey god, the other to Durga, the mother goddess. This is used every morning by the boys and younger men of the village for wrestling practice and physical exercises. To the west, beyond a field of maize, a red flag on a long stick rises out of a pile of whitened stones. This is the shrine of the gram deva or de Baba, the god who protects the village. Unlike Hanuman and Durga, he is not served by a brahmin priest but by a person of low caste whose home lies on the other side of the village, to the south.

Turning back from the recreation ground, walking past the dairymen's and brahmins' houses and across the tarmac road, one comes to another group of about forty small houses, all made of unburnt brick and with thatched roofs. A glance inside these houses

▼
5 Every Hindu house is a temple. Pictures and statues are placed on the household altar. Members of the family may pray at the shrine alone or together.

confirms one's first impression that they belong to people less well off than the rest of the villagers. They are clean and neat, but consist only of a kitchen and one other room. The kitchen contains earthenware and brass storage and cooking utensils, and the household shrine near the fireplace. The other room is empty except for the sleeping mats rolled up neatly in a corner. There is no table and no chairs. These are considered unnecessary luxuries by the people of this part of the village who are called chamars. They have their own tube well and work for the brahmins and dairymen, tending buffalo or looking after the fields. They have no land of their own. Chamars are traditionally leather workers by trade, often shoemakers, but the chamars of Ramdaspur have become farm labourers. Although this has not improved their status, they have become a little richer.

▶
6 Oxen are still important in the village economy but they are being displaced by tractors.

▼
7 Tractors and combine harvesters are becoming more and more a feature of Indian agriculture.

Shilur

Shilur lies in the south east of India, in Andhra Pradesh. It is a little bigger than Ramdaspur and very different, partly because it contains Christians and Muslims as well as Hindus.

Its Hindus are found in two groups. The brahmins and the merchant class, known as vaishyas, live on the north side of the road. Over a kilometre away, on the south side, are the washermen's families (the dhobis) and the barber caste (nai). Between these and the brahmins lie the homes of the Muslims with their mosque and the Christians with their small church. The Christians belong to low castes, being malas (agricultural labourers) or madigas (street sweepers) or scavengers. All of these groups have their own wells; none will touch water used by another group. The dhobis will not wash the clothes of the malas and madigas, not so much because they are Christians but because they eat meat. The vegetarian brahmins and vaishyas who own land and shops would not employ washermen who served non-vegetarians. The barbers cut the hair of every family in the village, but whereas they go to the houses of brahmins and vaishyas, the meat-eating Christians and Muslims, whom they regard as inferior in status, have to go to the barbers' own homes.

▼

8 Once rice fields depended totally upon water from rivers, streams and the monsoons. Now the tube wells which can be seen in the background provide more reliable supplies.

Vilayatpind

Our third village, Vilayatpind, is in the north of India, in Punjab. Its inhabitants are one hundred per cent leather-work caste. Yet the oldest of them cannot remember anyone working with leather, making shoes or tanning hides. They used to live by cultivating the fields of the rich landlords, known as Jats, whose village is two kilometres away. Now however, with government help, they have fields of their own and their own buffaloes and hens. They work for no one but themselves and are quite rich. Many sell their produce for cash in nearby Phagwara. Unlike the nearby Jat village, Vilayatpind has no television aerials so far and few of its houses are pukka (i.e. made of kiln-baked bricks), although each house does have its own pumped water. The Jats have now to employ migrant Hindu workers from Bihar or Uttar Pradesh to plant and harvest their rice, wheat and sugar cane. Vilayatpind has a small temple dedicated to the guru Ravidas.

TASKS TASKS TASKS TASKS TASKS TASKS

1 The daily routine begins early in an Indian village, even before sunrise, at 4.00 am in summer and 6.00 am in winter. Try to discover how members of different families might spend their day – the parents, sons and daughters of a brahmin family, a herdsman family, a washerman family and a barber family.

2 How might the lifestyle of a chamar in Punjab vary from that of a chamar in Ramdaspur?

3 Compile a scrapbook or make a frieze of photographs of Indians in their different regional costumes. You may also be able to obtain some costume cloth (Indian fabrics) and set up an exhibition. Link this exercise with things you did after reading unit 1.

4 Using clay, straw or pipecleaners for the figures, make models of Indians at work. Try to find out what style of clothes they would wear in Ramdaspur which is near Varanasi.

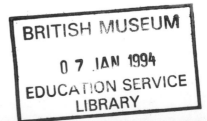

3
Caste

The word caste was introduced in the last chapter. It is now time to explain it. In order to do so, we really need to explain two words, varna and jati.

Varna

Varna literally means colour and is used to describe the four divisions of Hindu society. First there are the brahmins, the group from which the priests come though, as we have seen, not all brahmins earn a living as priests; many own land or run businesses. Indeed, they are to be found in most walks of life though never doing the kinds of work associated with shudras or outcastes. Being ritually pure brahmins often work in food businesses, perhaps owning restaurants.

The second group is called kshatriya. It was traditionally associated with the army and government but kshatriyas, like brahmins, are to be found today in most occupations. The same is true of the third varna, the vaishyas, though they are often found in some branch of commerce or trading and many shops and businesses are owned by them.

The shudras are the fourth order of Hindu society. Their traditional role was, and more often than not still is, that of serving the other three. The occupations associated with this varna are labouring in the fields, carrying water, pressing oil from vegetables, carpentry and making pots.

Outcastes

Beyond these four groups are the outcastes, those who are strictly speaking outside the Hindu system of life. This is what outcaste means literally. Why they are in this position cannot easily be explained. Hindus offer a variety of reasons. One is related to concepts of purity and pollution. Purity is not merely a matter of hygiene. We talk of cleansing the mind of evil thoughts, or washing our hands of a person or act, meaning we will have nothing to do with them. When a Hindu bathes it is not only to remove perspiration or dirt, it is also to get rid of any spiritual contamination which he or she may have picked up. Food is thought to pollute, especially the flesh and blood of an animal; which is why many Hindus are vegetarian. Water removes inner and outer taint, and some water is better than other for this purpose. The river Ganges is considered superior to any other, whereas, for example, the water that comes from the bathroom tap is thought inferior, no matter how carefully it has been filtered and treated with chemicals to remove bacteria. Purity and pollution extend to people. The brahmin is pure. At the other end of the scale is the outcaste. In the eyes of many brahmins, even the Ganges will not affect the impurity of outcastes. Belief in this permanent impurity means that they must live in another part of the village and use other wells lest contact with them should render the rest of the community temporarily impure. If one of these outcastes is employed as a servant, he or she may not enter the house, but must remain outside to wash the dishes which are placed by the pump or tap. When the outcaste has removed the remains of the meal from the plates and made them clean, a member of the brahmin family will rinse them again to take away pollution. No wonder these people have sometimes been called untouchables. Among the names they have been given, perhaps the best known is harijan, conferred on them by a famous twentieth-century Hindu called Mahatma Gandhi. It means 'children of God'. Gandhi once said that 'untouchability' is a crime against humanity! From its outset the government of independent India shared his view. Article 17 of the Indian Constitution abolished untouchability and forbade its practice in any form. By law, all have an equal right to draw water from any well, worship in any temple and enter any profession; all may own land and anyone has the same right of access to cafés, hotels and places of entertainment as anyone else.

Purity and pollution have to do with beliefs, so some scholars regard the caste system as religious in origin. Others claim that it was a method of social control used by a group of people called Aryans, who invaded India almost four thousand years ago. Certainly the outcastes have also been among the poorest members of Hindu society and have been victims of oppression. Despite the Indian Constitution the real status of many of them has not changed very much in the last thirty years. Some resent the

9 Mahatma Gandhi and one of the most famous women in the Indian freedom movement, Mrs Sarojini Naidu. At one time, when Gandhi was imprisoned, she became the movement's leader.

name harijan, regarding it as patronising. They call themselves dalit, oppressed, and have gone as far as publishing a journal by that name. This journal, written in the English language, appears fortnightly and aims to bring their plight to the notice of educated people and to influence public opinion. Traditionally, it was the outcastes who did the most unpleasant jobs, especially those of skinning dead animals and making shoes and other objects from their hides, sweeping the streets, and removing manure and other rubbish. Chamars (leather workers) and chuhras (sweepers) are the main outcaste groups, though they have other names in various parts of the country. Socially, other Hindus would not mix with them, one reason given being that they were the group most likely to contract and pass on disease. For them it was an occupational hazard.

Jati

A third way in which the caste system has been explained is in terms of economics. The tight social group called a jati has been the division that has mattered most in everyday life. Caste (jati) developed much later than class (varna); in fact evidence for it is not found until about 300 CE. It may have grown out of the varna system but could have an independent origin and have been absorbed into it later. Certainly, within each varna there are many jatis. Even among brahmins there are said to be 3000 different groups. Each jati keeps itself apart from the others to some degree, regarding them as capable of polluting its members ritually. In the past members of one jati did not eat with those of other jatis. They still rarely marry those outside their jati. Social relationships are determined by the fact that marriage is between members of different families but within the same jati. Employment too is governed by the jati, since its members have followed a hereditary occupation, though this is less so now than it was in the past. Goalas were dairymen, malis were farm labourers, telis traded in oil, jogis and jolahas were weavers. Sons pursued the occupation of their father, daughters married into homes where the trade of their father was followed, so that they were accustomed to the way of life and could be helpful in their husband's family. However, members of one jati have always either employed or worked for (depending on which belongs to the socially superior one) members of another jati, and the jatis have traded and done business with one another, not between their own members.

There is no doubt that the jati system has stabilised society and provided economic organisation. At the same time, by preventing movement, its effect is oppressive. Outcastes are not able to change their occupation; their children are denied educational opportunities. In this way they are exploited and condemned to remain dependent on the upper castes.

The position of outcastes today varies from place to place. It is possible to visit villages where everyone uses the same tube well for obtaining water and where there is a school which all children attend. The outcaste children as well as others go on to secondary school. Some make it to college or university and become doctors, teachers, social workers or business people. Often they remain in the towns, where there are most opportunities and where their caste background goes unknown and unnoticed. When they return home, they are respected by everyone and regarded as bringing honour to the whole village. They are, in particular, an example to children of their own jati by demonstrating what achievements are possible.

Obstacles can also be put in the way of people of low caste. For instance, a landowner might disapprove of the son of one of his labourers receiving an education and perhaps achieving more than his own son. He might tell the father that he expects the boy to come and work for him, as the family has done for generations, and that if he does not they will all have to start looking elsewhere for work. Faced with such threats the family would find it difficult to resist. If they complained to the police it would be far from easy to prove their allegations, especially against a rich, influential man.

The continuing influence of the caste system

The varna–jati system itself cannot change but in most areas of life its importance is slowly becoming less. There are some high-caste Hindus who continue to believe that contact with an outcaste pollutes them. Such people find life increasingly difficult. When they visit the cities they cannot be sure who will serve them in the shops. If they stay in their village they may be able to keep their way of life, but if they move outside it they cannot usually choose their work mates. However reluctant the most conservative brahmin may be, he is having to rethink his attitude to untouchability and acknowledge that it is no longer practicable.

Education can bring freedom for the low caste, though more so in the cities than in the villages. By outward appearance it is impossible to tell a person's traditional occupation or his varna. Skin colour is not the sure guide that some Hindus believe it to be. In the vastness of India it is possible to come across many South Indian brahmins who are darker than chamars of the Punjab, for example.

Wealth can also aid mobility but there is little evidence that conversion to one of those religions which claims to be opposed to caste discrimination helps. A sweeper may become a Christian, Muslim, Sikh, or Buddhist, but his social status will not be improved. In fact in the Punjab there is a special name, masahi, given to untouchables if they are Christian. It comes from the word 'Messiah' but means Christian untouchable.

Untouchables have tried to establish a separate, distinct identity through setting up their own new religious movements. One is the

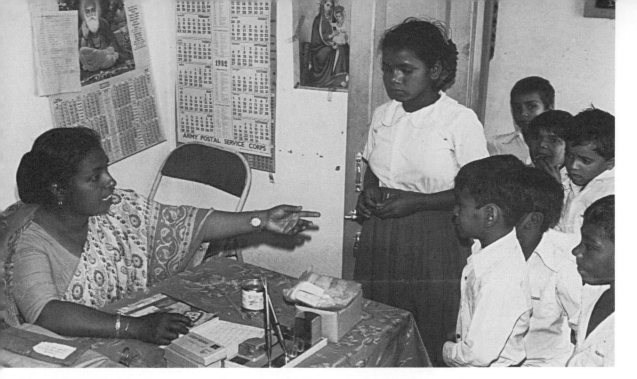

Valmiki Panth which looks upon the author of the *Ramayana*, one of Hinduism's sacred books, as its founder, inspirer and guru. Their headquarters is the temple of Ram Tirith in Amritsar where it is said Valmiki, who was a sweeper (chuhra), wrote his great epic. This movement is sometimes called the 'Balmiki Sabha', in Punjab. (In Punjabi Valmiki is pronounced with a 'B' at the beginning. Sabha means movement or association.) In some parts of Punjab the main village temple is dedicated to Valmiki.

A similar attempt has been made by the chamars; their leader is Guru Ravidas, a chamar saint poet who lived in the sixteenth century CE. They use as their holy book the *Guru Granth Sahib* of the Sikhs because it contains the hymns which Ravidas composed and many Ravidasis are Punjabi. Both chamars and chuhras have tried to persuade Hindu society that they are the original Hindus in the sense that they are the survivors and descendants of the first inhabitants of India, whereas the high-caste Hindus are descended from the invading Aryans who have only been in India for some three and a half thousand years! To make this point, the outcastes have sometimes called themselves Ad Dharmis. (Ad or Adi means original.) However, those who have claimed that theirs is the dharma (religion) of the first Indians have had little success in persuading the powerful majority.

A three-thousand-year-old system which has served India well and provides many benefits in the eyes of so many Hindus will not disappear overnight. Like much that is Indian it will, however, probably reshape itself in response to criticism both from outside and from within its own ranks.

▲
10 A woman headmistress—in education and as doctors, especially, women are playing an important part in the development of India. Whose pictures are on the wall?

▶ **11** Temple of Ram Tirith in the district of Amritsar.

TASKS TASKS TASKS TASKS TASKS TASKS

1 Find out what you can about Mahatma Gandhi's attitude to caste. To which varna did he belong? Which part of India did he come from?

2 List the benefits which the varna–jati system offers and the disadvantages. If you were a brahmin living in (a) New Delhi, (b) a village near Banares, what do you think your attitude to the system might be?

3 Imagine you are a brahmin. Write a letter to an English schoolboy explaining the varna–jati system.

4 What do you think this passage from the *Rig Veda* means?

When they divided primal Man,
How many divisions did they make?
What was his mouth? What his arms?
What were his thighs called? What his feet?

The brahmin was his mouth,
The kshatriya his arm,
His thighs the vaishya,
The shudra came from his feet.

RIG VEDA, Book 10, hymn 90

5 Jati is most important nowadays when it comes to arranging marriages. Can you think why? Check your answer against reasons given in the next chapter.

4
Hindu family life

At first glance family life may not appear to be a religious matter but this is to view it from a very western standpoint. If we do that we shall never make head or tail of Hinduism – or even of Indian Christianity. All Indian families are extended families in at least one of two ways. Firstly, however westernised they have become, they are close-knit, regularly in contact, and very concerned about every member's wellbeing. It is rare to find that relatives, even distant cousins, have lost touch with one another. Secondly, the extended family members usually live together or very near one another. In many towns as well as villages many will be found living together under one roof.

The size of extended families is virtually limitless. A few years ago a family was discovered with over six hundred members. It was really a family village with its own school and dispensary. More common is the household which comprises father and mother, married sons and their wives and children, unmarried daughters and perhaps father's and occasionally mother's parents, who are too old to look after themselves. In the family everyone has a part to play. This may be less obvious in the city, where the men and some of the women probably have paid jobs, than in the countryside where there is greater interaction. Here the able-bodied men will look after any land that the family may own; otherwise they will work for a traditional employer. At busy times, younger sons and the women will lend a hand. However, the chief occupation of the women will be providing food and cooking it, or selling produce if they have milk or cheese to take to market. In the home there is always plenty to be done. It is usually grandma who keeps the smaller children who are not at school from under the feet of their mother and busy brothers and sisters. She will tell them stories and take them to the village temple if there is one and if she goes to it. She will also make her own act of worship at the family shrine which will be in the house, probably in the kitchen. The children will learn their Hinduism from her.

In Hindi there is a special name for each of the relatives you are likely to meet. So you would have no problem deciding how to distinguish between mum's sister Betty and dad's, or between one set of grandparents and the other. The language does it for you. This is a short list of Hindi terms which Pushpa, the daughter of the family, might use.

Bap – *father*
Ma(n) (pronounced with a slightly nasalised 'n' sound) – *mother*
Dada and dadi – *paternal grandfather and grandmother*
Nana and nani – *maternal grandfather and grandmother*
Chacha and chachi – *uncle (father's brother) and aunt (wife of father's brother)*
Phuphi and phua – *aunt (father's sister) and uncle (husband of father's sister)*
Mama and mami – *uncle (mother's brother) and aunt (wife of mother's brother)*
Mausi and mausa – *aunt (mother's sister) and uncle (husband of mother's sister)*

Pushpa will call an older brother bhai and an older sister bahi(n). She will address her younger brothers and sisters by their given name; of course they will not call her Pushpa, but bahi(n). Often 'ji' is added to a name as a sign of affection, for example 'chachaji'. Children are given pet names which their relatives may use. The use of names denotes a hierarchy of relationships in Hindu families.

The family also has a head – usually the senior male member. When he dies, the family will meet after a period of mourning to invest someone else with his authority. The head will be consulted on all important matters, for example the arrangement of marriages or the further education of children, and it is he who settles any disputes which may arise between one section of the family and another.

Hierarchy extends throughout the family and can be observed during meals. The senior male members of the family will eat first, then the boys and the women. In a small household of, say, father, mother and two sons, a visitor might find himself eating with the father and eldest son and being waited on by a younger son, even though that son may be eighteen years old. Mother will be busy preparing the meal. Of course there are many homes now where everyone sits down together for a meal and shares the domestic chores – directed, needless to say, by the senior woman!

Sons are considered far more important to a family than

daughters. There are a number of reasons for this. First, for most Indians there are no old age pensions, so parents depend on their children when they become too old or infirm to care for themselves. Sons remain within the family, but daughters leave home when they marry and become members of another family. Their parents cannot appeal to them for help. Secondly, sons are more able to go out to work than daughters, whose role has been to help mother with the domestic aspect of household life. Thirdly, the eldest son has an important part to play in the welfare of his parents when they die. At their cremations there are certain prayers and rituals which the eldest son should carry out in order to speed their souls to the next life. Though a son may be adopted to carry out these functions, parents naturally prefer their own offspring to perform the last rites. Once again we must note that the tradition is changing. Daughters often keep in touch with their parents as much as sons and there are dutiful sons-in-law who care for them with as much affection as their own sons. There are also Hindu women following careers in most professions and earning as much as their brothers. Although the traditional lot of women in Hindu society has often been unsatisfactory and far from pleasant, it is important to remember that this has been the lot of women in most cultures. Besides, it was possible for a Hindu woman, Mrs Gandhi, to become her country's Prime Minister. Nevertheless, traditions die hard. The desire and need for sons remains, making the struggle of family planning agencies to encourage birth control extremely difficult. The tradition of giving a dowry when a girl marries also means that she is an expense to the family. The practice is illegal but custom and family pride help to preserve it.

Marriage

Hindu marriages are arranged marriages. Occasionally it is possible to find a couple who met at work or college, fell in love and married, with or without their parents' consent, but frequently such couples have had to detach themselves from the extended family and make their own way.

Arranged marriages are necessary in India. None of the Indian languages has a word that can be used to say that a member of the opposite sex is one's friend. Friendship is expected to be confined to one's own sex. Small children play happily together but before they reach puberty the two sexes go their separate ways. There is co-education in secondary schools, colleges and

Two Hindu people meeting

universities, but in class there is no mixing and outside class boys walk and talk with boys and girls with girls. When people meet and greet one another with the Hindu word 'Namaste' or 'Namaskar', which really means 'I bow respectfully to you', there is no physical contact between the sexes. People do not usually shake hands; certainly men do not normally shake the hands of women, nor do couples hold each other's hands or kiss in public. Hand-shaking has been adopted by westernised Hindus in India and by many living in Britain.

It is considered vital to the family that a marriage should be arranged with great care. One individual is not merely marrying another; he or she is marrying an extended family. It is important that the girl's parents should choose a good husband for their daughter because she is going to move away from home and they want her to be happy. They will therefore take care to seek someone with a similar background to their own.

The son's family may be more anxious to make a good choice. A stranger, the bride, is going to enter their household. It is essential that she fits in as easily as possible. The mother-in-law to be will be especially anxious not to have a daughter with modern independent city ways, always wanting to go to the cinema or to discos when she should be helping in the house, eager to follow her career when she should be providing grandsons!

The whole family may be involved in the task of searching and matching: the father perhaps making it known that he considers the particular child ready for marriage; a brother then telling the father that one of his wife's relatives is looking for a marriage partner for their child. After informal soundings have been taken the serious business may begin. The formalities used to be left to the barber but this practice is much less common now. Families of higher castes have sometimes employed brahmins as matchmakers (ghatakas). Whatever the procedure, a comparison of the horoscopes will definitely be considered necessary at some stage.

The saying 'marriages are made in heaven' expresses the literal truth for many Hindus. They do not see life as something that takes place on earth for a period of seventy or eighty years unrelated to anything else. It is part of a cosmic process which has links with the past and the future as well as with worlds beyond this planet. When arranging a marriage, it is as important to take into consideration the moment of birth – the position of the stars, sun and moon at that time – as it is for the couple to belong to the same jati. In former times, once the match was decided, the couple would not meet again until the wedding ceremony; now practices vary. In many cases they do meet before the betrothal takes place, but they will be chaperoned. When the date and time of the wedding have been fixed by astrologers, the invitations will be sent out. Love matches are not usual in India.

The wedding

Some months are more popular than others for Hindu weddings. Spring, when the weather is still cool, is the best time of all. There is only one forbidden period, in the month of Aswin (October), when Hindus should keep their dead ancestors in mind, fasting rather than enjoying themselves.

The wedding may take place at almost any hour of the day or night, depending on the time determined by the astrologer. It is a joyful affair, with everyone turning up in their best clothes, often new ones bought specially for the occasion. It is also costly, especially for the bride's family, not only because it happens at her home and her parents bear the cost of the ceremony and meal, but also because her father will probably have agreed to give a dowry. Although this is now an illegal practice in India most families probably ignore the law for one reason or another. A father will often consider it a matter of pride not to send away his daughter empty-handed. However, marriages do take place in which neither caste nor dowry play any part.

The wedding is also likely to be a noisy affair with bands playing, people singing and fire crackers going off to let everyone know what is happening.

12 A Hindu couple make their marriage vows under the direction of a priest.

The focus of the wedding is the fire representing God in the form of Agni, the one who purifies and takes the prayers and offerings of devout Hindus to heaven. When the groom's party has arrived and been greeted with food and gifts, the bride's father will take her hand and place it on the hand of the groom who will say, 'I accept you.' After this short but important ceremony, the couple are taken to their places on the north side of the fire facing the priest. The rest of the guests will be already seated behind and to the side of the priest. Bride and groom should not look at each other at this time. They are screened from one another by a red curtain or sheet. Songs are sung and the guests throw rice at the couple to wish them happiness and prosperity.

When the curtain is removed the couple garland one another with sweetly scented flowers. The groom is instructed by the priest to throw certain things, such as rice, nuts and ghee (liquified butter) into the fire while prayers are said. The bride, sitting on the left of the groom, shares in this act by touching his right shoulder as he makes the oblations. To the bride he says,

'I am the sun, you are the earth. May my seed planted in you produce children. May they outlive us. May we love and admire one another and protect one another with a kind heart. May we see, hear and live a hundred autumns.'

Making a further three offerings of roasted rice or maize the couple stand as the groom says,

'I free this bride from obligations to her father's family. Now they are to her husband's family. Now she stands securely bound to her husband. May we be blessed with worthy offspring.'

The end of the bride's sari that hangs over her shoulder is then tied to the scarf which the husband is wearing. The wedding knot has been tied. It should never be undone. Strict Hinduism has no place for divorce, though it is possible under Indian law. The couple now proceed seven times round the sacred fire with the groom leading. The saptapedi, or seven steps, are accompanied by these words spoken by the groom:

O my bride, take the first step to acquire strength.
Take the second step for power.
Take the third step for wealth and prosperity.
Take the fourth step for happiness.
Take the fifth step for children.
Take the sixth step for the enjoyment of pleasure.
Take the seventh step for the closeness of our union.

They then sit down side by side, the bride on the groom's left. After more prayers, if the wedding is at night, the husband will take his wife outside, turn north and point out the Pole Star to her. She says,

'The Pole Star is Dhruva, constant. May I be Dhruva in my husband's family.'

When this ceremony of Dhruva-Darshan has been completed, everyone's attention turns to the wedding feast. However poor the family, no expense is spared in providing a sumptuous meal – something which will impress the guests, especially the groom's family, and give the daughter a memorable send-off. When she leaves with her husband she will take her dowry with her, if there is one, though nowadays it may be sent separately. She will go to the home of her husband's parents where she has at least one further small ceremony to perform: before entering the house, she must kick over a metal pot containing wheat with her right foot. It will have been placed so that when she knocks it over the grain will fall across the threshold into the house. It signifies that she brings prosperity. Before setting out to claim his bride, the young man will probably have visited the various village shrines. Now he will go again, accompanied by his bride.

They will make offerings of rice balls as they pray for a long and happy life. Though the young bride may feel nervous and perhaps lonely in her new surroundings, her new sisters, cousins and other women of the village who may make the rounds with them will sing and dance, making it a happy occasion.

Now the girl is married she will wear the signs of a Hindu wife: a necklace of black beads on a gold thread with two pieces of gold, semi-circular in shape, placed amid the beads. A married lady whose husband is alive wears a red dot on her forehead. This must not be confused with the mark that the priest puts on the forehead of all who have attended temple worship.

Ceremonies of childhood

Hinduism can be extremely ritualistic. Few Hindus today have the time or money to perform all the rituals and some would regard many of them as belonging to a bygone era and no longer necessary. For example, in the past when a woman was about to give birth, she might be put in a darkened room away from the rest of the family, with only the midwife for company, so that no evil spirits reach her or the child. The separation was probably sensible, a wise precaution against germs and disease – but other medical aids are now available. Altogether there are at least sixteen rites which are generally observed, beginning before birth and ending with prayers for deceased ancestors.

Child-naming

The first of these 'sanskars' as they are called, which is commonly performed, has to do with birth and child-naming. This should take place on the sixth day after the birth of the baby.

On this day the mother may bathe for the first time after giving birth. She will be given new clothes and the house will be filled with fresh flowers. The father, who must not have shaved since the baby was born, will now remove his growth of hair. The whole emphasis is on the removal of pollution, and on renewal. The priest may come to cast the baby's horoscope and help with name choosing. This he does by using the horoscope to determine what the initial letter of the name should be. The name is never given lightly or because it sounds nice, though it has to be admitted that sometimes children are called after film stars! (India's cinema industry is the biggest in the world.) However, all names have a meaning and for the Hindu it should be that that counts. Most Hindus know what their name means.

Upanayana

The most important ceremony for a Hindu of one of the upper three varnas is the thread-giving rite. Members of the brahmin, kshatriya and vaishya classes are known as twice born, dvija. To enter upon full membership of their class they must be initiated. The Hindu word for the initiation is upanayana. Long ago the ceremony marked a young man's entry upon the first of the four stages of Hindu life. These were: studentship; householder, when he married; renunciate, when he handed over his responsibilities to his sons; and recluse, when he left even his wife and went to live by himself – homeless, wandering in the forest. There he spent his time preparing for death and the final liberation of his spirit.

On the day when the upanayana is to be performed, relatives and guests gather at the home of the boy, who is probably between eight and ten years of age. He will only be given milk to drink for breakfast; then, in the presence of the guests, he will have his head shaved except for a small tuft. He is now ready to say farewell to his past life and become a Hindu. Dressed only in a loin-cloth, he will be brought by his father to the sacred fire, where offerings will be made. A white cord made of three threads of cotton will be hung over the boy's left shoulder and under his right arm. This janeu should be worn day and night throughout the rest of his life. Each year it should be renewed at a special ceremony in Bhrapada (September), called Ganesha Chaturti, Ganesha's birthday.

The initiate takes a vow of celibacy and the priest whispers the most sacred Hindu verse of scripture in his ear, the Gayatri Mantra. It reads,

> We meditate on the lovely light of the God, Savitri: may it stimulate our thoughts.

Savitri is the sun-god, but of course the prayer is not for sunny days but for inner illumination, spiritual enlightenment.

In past times the boy would leave his family and head for a quiet place in the forest to live with a guru, a spiritually enlightened teacher who would educate him in sacred knowledge. He would remain with his guru until the teacher thought him ready to return to his parents, be freed from his vows and be married. One myth tells of someone who took a hundred years to complete this student stage of life! Nowadays the boy takes a staff in his hand and makes as if to leave home, but stays to enjoy the party and receive presents and the congratulations of relatives.

A Hindu funeral

▼ ▶
13, 14 Hindu cremation scenes: an old man's body is carried by his relatives in a procession through the streets to the burning ground. In India cremations take place out of doors and relatives prepare the pyre and perform the rituals, including lighting it.

Death comes at last, a man may hope after the best part of a hundred autumns have been enjoyed and when the declining years have been made happy by the appearance of grandchildren. The future of the family, the preservation of the family name, the care of the grandmother is now assured. The old man can die in peace. Even though he is a twice born, he will not have gone away from home to live out the last stage of his life, but he will probably have put aside his worldly cares and taken to giving more time to meditation, to studying the scriptures, to making offerings at the household shrine and perhaps to going on pilgrimages. His priorities

will have become what he was told they should be at his upanayana ceremony: studying the scriptures and seeking enlightenment and spiritual liberation.

It is customary to cremate a Hindu on the day of death, unless that takes place in the evening. The body is washed and wrapped in cloth – white is usually used for men though not so generally for women. Then it is put on a stretcher and carried by relatives through the town to the burning ground. It is customary for large cities to have municipal grounds where piles of wood stand ready and assistants are available to help the relatives. In villages there is simply an area of land which is used for no other purpose, the mourners have to carry the materials for the funeral pyre with them. In town and country the cremation is carried out by relatives and friends. This gives the bereaved the satisfaction of being fully involved in the last rites and in helping the spirit on its way to a better life.

In the procession that winds its way after the stretcher the men go first, the women walk some way behind. As the men approach the ground they say, 'Rama's name is the name of truth. Such is the fate of all men.' At the place of cremation sticks are neatly set down, almost like a bed. The body is laid on them and more pieces of wood are piled on top. Most of the men share in this act of devotion. Ghee is put amid the sticks. It is a purifying agent but it also helps the pyre to burn more quickly. Sometimes a brahmin is present to guide the son or chief mourner as he conducts the rites; otherwise, friends or relatives who have experienced this occasion before, or the attendants, will instruct him. The body will have been placed with its feet facing south towards the realm of the god of death, Yama. The fire is lit first at the north end but the son will carry the burning brand, a stick with a rag covered in pitch, to other parts of the pyre. When it is alight nuts, rice and other offerings are thrown into the flames while prayers are said. The party stays watching until the fire begins to subside and it is clear that the deceased's body has been consumed.

After the funeral the mourners will bathe and change their clothes. Two or three days later the son comes back to the cremation ground to recover the ashes which will be taken to a river and scattered in the water. Sometimes they will be kept at home until it is convenient for someone to take them to the most sacred of all rivers, the Ganges, perhaps at Allahabad where three rivers meet. For ten days the family is in deep mourning, keeping itself very much to itself. During this time further rituals for the dead are performed until the final shradda ceremony some time after the tenth day. However, it must be remembered that each year, during the shradda days in late September or early October, in the month of Bhrapada, the family always offers prayers for its ancestors.

The lot of most Hindus is to die in their home or in hospital but the ideal is to die at Banares (now called Varanasi), the sacred city on the west bank of the Ganges. If they die between the twin rivers of the Varun and the Asi which flow through the city into the Ganges it is said they will not be reborn again. Some old people, as they feel death approaching, make a last pilgrimage to the city and wait there to die.

TASKS TASKS TASKS TASKS TASKS TASKS

1 Make a collage of a Hindu wedding.

2 List reasons why arranged marriages are normal in all religious communities in India.

3 If a typical British family, not religious, were to arrange a marriage for

   a its son
   b its daughter

what factors would it be interested In?

   Christians have arranged marriages in some parts of the world. What concerns might Christian parents have in choosing a partner for their child? What concerns might Hindu parents have in choosing a husband wife for their child?

In response to a survey of beliefs people in Britain replied as follows:

38% said they believed in life after death, 35% said they did not; 23% expressed belief in hell, 58% did not; 54% believed in heaven, 27% did not; 18% believed in rebirth, 52% did not. The rest of the people questioned said they were uncertain.

Put these figures into four bar graphs entitled 'Life After Death: Hell: Heaven: Rebirth'.

Conduct your own class or school survey and put the results into four bar graphs. How do the results compare with the national survey?

5 Religious people believe in life after death as a matter of faith, but how might a Hindu argue in favour of life beyond death? What reasons might be given for believing in rebirth?

6 Hindus do not regard rebirth as a second chance but as something to be avoided if at all possible. How can it be avoided? Why might it be considered undesirable?

7 What changes in funeral customs have Hindus living in Britain had to make? Why? Why might they find these changes distressing?

5
God, worship and festivals

How many gods are there? This is the question that many people ask as they look up at the great gateway towers of the temple of Meenakshi at Madurai in south India. They stand forty-eight metres high. Even when you have climbed one hundred and fifty steps and you look out of one of the windows six storeys up, you are still not at the top. The faces of these immense towers are covered with carvings. These are of human beings, animals, birds, reptiles and some creatures which only exist in the imagination, but almost all of them are representations of God.

▶

16 A Hindu bathing at the Meenakshi Temple, Madurai, before offering puja. Note the massive temple gateways.

When a child once asked how many gods there were, he was given the answer: three hundred and thirty-three million. Most of them seem to be visible at Madurai. Despite this, some Hindus will say there is one God and others will say that there is none at all. How can such different replies be explained?

One man, when asked to explain the belief in many gods, did it in this way. He began by putting a question to the questioner: 'How many people do you think there are in the world?' he said. 'About three thousand million,' came the reply. 'And how many animals and birds?' 'I don't know. Millions, I suppose,' was the answer given. 'Well, we Hindus believe that the life in them is God. So there are as many gods as there are creatures. But the life principle is the same, so you see we believe in many gods, and one God, at the same time.'

Some Hindus are atheists. They would say that there is no God. Life simply exists. It always has and it always will. Existence is self-explanatory. There is no need to introduce the idea of God to make sense of the universe or to give purpose to individual lives. It is possible to be a Hindu and not believe in God.

To return to the carvings on the temple gateways at Madurai,

▲

17 A gateway (gopuram) of the Meenakshi Temple, Madurai, showing Shiva and Parvati as well as other figures of Hinduism.

what was the purpose of those who made them? We cannot be sure but they took their inspiration from Hindu mythology and were trying perhaps to give pilgrims a warning. It is so easy to say we know something. We know our mathematical tables, we know how to spell, we know how to find our way around London, or Delhi, or Bombay, or New York. The pilgrim might even arrive at Madurai thinking 'I know God'. So the craftsman used his art to issue a challenge, 'Which God do you know?' Hopefully, the pilgrim would become humble and acknowledge that human beings cannot comprehend the divine.

Brahman

Some religions, Judaism, Islam and Sikhism for example, refuse to depict God through pictures. Instead they use words. When speaking of God, Muslims use ninety-nine names, besides Allah, which is simply the Arabic for 'God', meaning the one God. 'Compassionate', 'merciful', 'great' are three of them. Jews and Christians use words like Father, the Holy One, the Lord. A verse of a Christian hymn contains many of these names.

> Immortal, invisible, God only wise,
> In light inaccessible hid from our eyes,
> Most blessèd, most glorious, the ancient of days,
> Almighty, victorious, thy great name we praise.

Hindus use pictures as well as words. By using many pictures they hope to communicate the immensity and variety which is God. They also give God many names. For the Hindu god is represented as female as well as male. Yet beyond all this variety the Hindu knows that God is one. As the oldest of the world's scriptures, the *Rig Veda*, puts it,

> Ekam sat vipra bahuda vadantyagnim yaman matarishvanamahuh
> To what is one sages give many a name, Agni, Yama, Matarisvan

Book 1, hymn 164, verse 46

The *Yajur Veda*, a slightly later text, comments on this verse as follows,

> For an awakened soul, Indra, Varuna, Agni, Yama, Aditya, Chandra, all these names represent only one basic power and spiritual entity.

The earliest parts of the *Rig Veda* may be three and a half thousand years old. The verse quoted above is probably only three thousand years old. So, long ago the people who later came to be called Hindus believed in one basic power and spiritual entity. Their name for it is Brahman.

In Indian languages words can be masculine, feminine or neuter. 'Brahman' is neuter. God, the Ultimate Reality, lies outside and beyond the notions of male and female. However, when Brahman is broken down into the three hundred and thirty-three million gods, many of them are goddesses and others are animals and birds. Over the centuries there have been rises and falls in the importance of different deities. Indra, for example, was one of the main gods worshipped about three thousand years ago, but in a story originating about five hundred years later he has become almost a figure of fun. The story tells how, when he had been initiated with the sacred thread, he proved such a poor brahmacharya that he had to spend a hundred and one years with his teacher! His guru, Prajapati, must have been extremely patient. Nowadays Hindus learn about Indra in books rather than worshipping him.

With the passage of time and the changes it has brought about, a number of deities have come to the fore. Often they are mentioned in pairs, the god and his female consort, or in threes, including the bird or animal creature which is always associated with the pair.

A god who is found in most stories, and whose statue or picture is a common feature of temples, is Brahma, yet it is said only six temples in the whole of India are dedicated to him. He is regarded as the god who presided over the creation of the universe. His job, so some Hindus will say, is done so why worship him? Others see the process of creation as continual. Change is a fact of life. We grow old and die, new creatures take our place. Brahma's work is never at an end. However, his consort, Saraswati, the goddess of learning, receives more attention than Brahma, especially from students about to sit examinations. The creature associated with Brahma and Saraswati is the swan.

Vishnu

The busiest of the gods must be Vishnu, the preserver. According to Hindu mythology he takes many forms to accomplish his never-ending task. He may incarnate himself as an animal or a human being in order to defeat the forces of evil. In one story he disguises himself as a dwarf first to deceive and then to defeat a demon who has gained control of the world. No one could overthrow the demon, Bali, and his allies, so Vishnu left his heavenly abode, turned himself into a dwarf and presented himself in the presence

◄

18 Vishnu in his ten incarnations: Matsya the fish; Kurma the tortoise; Varaha the boar; Narasimha the man-lion; Vamana the dwarf; Parasurama, 'Rama with the axe'; Rama the prince; Krishna; Buddha; and Kalki.

of Bali. He asked Bali to grant him a favour. The demon, who was in a good mood, agreed. 'I would like all the land that I can cover in three strides,' said the dwarf. Looking at him, the demon felt he had no cause for fear. 'So be it,' he replied. At this, the dwarf, whose energy surpassed that of the sun, assumed his divine form. With one step he strode over the earth, with another the heavens, and with his third the whole universe. Evil, in the form of Bali, had been defeated. This may not appear to be a particularly moral tale. The god practised deceit upon the demon. However, the fault lay with Bali. If he had not been so caught up with his own importance, if he had been properly aware as he should have been, he would have recognised the god who stood in front of him, even in the form of a dwarf. Ignorance is not an excuse in Hindu teachings.

Rama

Perhaps the most famous incarnation – or avatar, as Hindus say – is Rama. He took birth in order to rid the world of another demon, Ravana, the king of Lanka. Rama became king of a place called Ayodhya in northern India. There he lived happily with his wife Sita until one day, when he was away on a hunting expedition, Ravana abducted her. Rama searched for her for fourteen years without success until the king of the monkeys, Hanuman, discovered where she was from his spies. The armies of Hanuman and Rama combined to rescue the queen and restore her safely to her palace. Just as Rama is another form of Vishnu, so Sita is really Lakshmi, goddess of wealth and Vishnu's consort. Associated with them is Garuda, the king of the birds, vulture-like in appearance.

Krishna

Krishna is another extremely popular incarnation of Vishnu. Hindus travel from all over the world to visit his birthplace at Mathura on the river Jumna. His statue is to be found in many temples. Whereas Rama carries a bow, Krishna can be recognised by the flute which he holds to his lips. With this he charmed the girls who looked after the cattle, including his consort, Radha, who usually stands at his side. He inspires, and gives, love. Many stories portray him as a naughty boy or an attractive young man winning the hearts of the cowgirls, but the purpose of these is to remind his worshippers that God is loving and loveable. He draws people to him by his loving grace and through it helps them to face life and successfully overcome their problems. Krishna is also the main character in the most famous of Hindu scriptures, the *Bhagavad Gita*. There he appears to be only a charioteer, but eventually his master, the prince Arjuna, recognises him to be the supreme God, Brahman, and worships him.

Shiva

Shiva is often regarded as the destructive aspect of divinity, but this is an over-simplification as is much about Hinduism. The act of destruction is itself an act necessary for creation to take place. Out of the destructive force of a volcano new islands may be formed, from the levelling of existing buildings a new town may emerge. In Hindu thinking, the processes of destruction and creation belong together.

Shiva does not usually appear as an avatar – that is a special feature of Vishnu – but he helps when humanity is faced by a catastrophe. One story links him with the river Ganges. It is said that a great sage Kapila had killed the sixty thousand sons of a king, Sagara, with a glance that had turned them to ashes. Water was needed to purify their remains but there was a great drought and none was available. When an appeal was made to Vishnu, he said that he could persuade the goddess Ganga to descend upon the earth in the form of a river, but there was one problem – descending as she would from heaven, the force would smash the earth to smithereens! Reluctantly, for he hated to admit that there could be anyone greater than himself, Vishnu conceded that Shiva might be able to help. Now Shiva is known as the great yogi, one who can control immense power through the discipline of meditation. When the saint Bhagiratha approached him, he agreed to sit in his yogic posture, take the force of the water upon his head and allow it to run down his body to the earth. This he did, and that is how the world's most holy river became available to humanity. Of course, this story is told by devotees of Shiva who want to say that he is the greatest of the gods. His wife is Parvati, but she is known by many other names: Uma, Durga, Kali being just a few of the most famous. The animal associated with Shiva is the bull Nandi, found guarding the entrance to most of his temples.

The mother goddess, the divine in female form, is one of the most important features of Hinduism. If God is all life, present within all living beings, then half of life is female, so it is only natural to represent God as female as well as male. As Lakshmi, Saraswati or Sita, she possesses the characteristics customarily associated with womanhood – beauty, wisdom and fidelity – but as the consort of Shiva she can be strong-willed, powerful, even fierce. The demure image of Indian womanhood is less than half the picture, as anyone who has lived in a Hindu household or seen women working in a village knows.

Ganesha or Ganupati

One more deity must be added to our list: Ganesha, often called Ganupati. This is the pot-bellied, elephant-headed son of Shiva and Parvati. How Ganesha came to have an elephant's head is not certain. There is a story that tells of Shiva coming to the palace of his consort and being given their young child to nurse. His consort was none too pleased when the baby's head fell off. To make amends Shiva sent Nandi to find a replacement. This would be the first creature he came across lying down with his head facing north.

◀

19 Ganesha in the Meenakshi Temple which is dedicated to his mother, Parvati. Meenakshi, meaning 'fish-eyed', is one of Parvati's names.

39

After some time, Nandi came upon the king of the elephants sleeping with his head to the north, so he struck off his head with his sword and carried it back to Shiva who placed it on the shoulders of his son. Who can tell what the origin of the tale is? What is known is that for some reason Ganesha is called the remover of obstacles. At the beginning of all important undertakings and acts of worship he is always invoked.

Temples and temple worship

Hindu temples in India vary. They are buildings to contain a holy object which worshippers venerate. They can be so small that there is scarcely room for the priest who attends the shrine to enter. In such cases the devotee has to stand outside on the other side of the threshold, but this does not matter. Nor should it matter what the worshipper brings. The god Krishna, in one of the most famous Hindu scriptures, the *Bhagavad Gita*, says:

> Whatever a zealous soul may offer,
> Be it a leaf, a flower, fruit, or water,
> That I willingly accept
> For it was given in love.
>
> Chapter 9, verse 26

It is the attitude of the giver that is important, not the gift. Flowers are precisely what many people give. They may bring a single one in the hand, or they may place a garland of saffron-coloured marigolds or red roses around the neck of the deity or over the frame of the picture. It is not unusual to see a woman with a bunch of flowers going from temple to temple down a street, putting one flower from the bunch in front of each statue. Before dawn she will have risen from her bed, bathed, gathered her flowers, or bought them from the flower-sellers who have already set up their pitches by six o'clock, and be on her way making her devotions. Only when they are completed will she go home to make breakfast.

All the larger, more popular shrines will be attended by a priest. He need not be a person trained in theology. It is his job to attend the deity and conduct the appropriate rituals. When the worshippers come he will receive their offerings and give them prasad. This is a sign of God's grace; it represents the blessing which the deity gives the devotees. It may take the form of a piece of fruit, some nuts or raisins, or a piece of crystallised sugar. What the worshipper offers, the priest usually keeps. It constitutes his wages. Sometimes, therefore, he is eager to receive gifts of money rather than food. Some of these priests are the descendants of brahmins who have looked after the shrines for more years than anyone can remember. Deep devotion, family pride and respect for the gods are all involved. If the priest is a middle-aged man, he may never have been to school. It is likely that he was taught by his father to read and write. His father will also have trained him in the service of the shrine and its worshippers. A Hindu with personal problems would not go to the priest but to members of his family. Those who have theological difficulties or like to discuss religion can find elders in the village who enjoy talking about religion – it is a popular topic of conversation in India – or they can go to gurus or wise men called swamis. We shall come across these again shortly.

Most towns have large temples, as do religiously important villages like Vrindaban where Krishna was born. These temples fall into two main types. After visiting a number of each kind one begins to recognise the similarities.

Open temples

First there is the temple which is open to the sky. It lies behind high walls built centuries ago to protect it from intruders, when Muslim armies might raid and destroy it. The Muslims have often regarded Hindus as worshippers of idols. Now the communities live together more happily, but the old walls remain.

On entering the temple through one of its gate towers the worshipper finds himself in a large paved area like a courtyard. Directly in front of him will be a number of small temples with their attendant priests. One of these shrines will certainly be dedicated to Ganesha, the remover of obstacles, the deity invoked at the beginning of any act of worship. Naturally one's worship in the temple begins with him. Going left – one always travels round a temple clockwise – we would come upon other shrines. Some are like that of Ganesha, cube-shaped, with dimensions of about three metres In each direction, length, breadth and height. They would be white, made either of stone or marble. Beyond the entrance where the priest would be sitting or standing, is the statue of the god. It might be no more than a metre and a half high, standing on a plinth, or it might be quite tall, almost three metres from base to top. Occasionally we would come across a statue built into a wall or open to the sky.

Visitors generally worship in front of each statue in turn on their journey round the temple, perhaps pausing longer at some than at others. They pause longest at those of the best-known deities or the ones for which their family has had a traditional reverence.

Eventually visitors will reach the most important deity of the temple, standing in the largest shrine, situated in the centre of the complex. This will be as big as most domestic houses. The god will be in a room at the end of a passage. The room will be lit by candles or the light from clay oil-lamps. Probably three or four priests will be in attendance. The tall statue would be visible from the entrance if we could see beyond the crowds of pilgrims making their way along the entry passage. In the half-darkness it is an awesome sight. If we joined the worshippers, once we had reached the shrine room we would either bow or prostrate ourselves fully, which might be difficult with the crowds milling around; however, the devotee takes no notice of anyone but the object of his or her devotion, the god, and beyond that, God.

After offering prayers and fruit, flowers or money, and receiving prasad from the priest, we would walk around the god. Enough room is always left at the side and the back, as well as the front, for worshippers to walk around inside, just as they do outside at the other shrines.

Blinking, and possibly shivering for a moment as we come back into the open air, we follow the other men, women and children, on our clockwise journey, bowing or prostrating ourselves as we come to other shrines. Finally we are back at the entrance. During our visit we shall not have come across a single act of congregational worship. Like everyone else, we shall have been doing our own thing. To a very large extent, Hindu religious belief and practice is an individual matter. Many Hindus never go to a temple. Either they worship the gods in their house shrines or they practise no rituals, preferring to meditate or study the scriptures.

Back outside the temple, we collect our shoes from a little place that every major temple has where shoes are left in the care of volunteer attendants and we go on our way. If we are thirsty or hungry we can buy food or drink from one of the many stalls near the temple gate.

Enclosed temples

The other kind of temple is fully enclosed. In fact, however, it is many temples housed under one roof. Its main entrance faces the rising sun. At the top of the flight of steps which we climb to enter the temple, there is a huge bell hanging over the doorway. Worshippers reach up to the rope hanging from it, pull the rope and announce their coming to God. Probably most of the shrines in the

20 Shiva lingam at The Hindu University, Varanasi.

other temple had their bells, but they were not so prominently placed so we did not notice them.

We walk along the marble-paved corridors, keeping always to the left, of course, and come to side rooms here and there, where statues of gods stand. Worshippers enter each in turn to make their offerings and receive prasad. On the inner walls of some of these temples we may find paintings of religious scenes, or pictures made of coloured pieces of marble. Sometimes there are verses from the scriptures, written in the sacred language, Sanskrit, in one of the regional languages or in English.

In a large room in the centre of the building there will be the main shrine with its attendant priest. In new temples of the kind we are describing the room is likely to be bright and airy, lit by windows and electricity rather than by candles and wick lamps.

Where possible modern temples, certainly if they are of the large kind, have lawns and planted gardens around them. Those in cities often have to compete for space with houses and shops. From the road all that tells the passer-by that the building is a temple is the gateway, though this may be unremarkable, and the sound of chanting at certain times of the day.

Hindus may go to the temple at almost any time of day and on any day in the week. There is no special day set aside as there is in some other religions, such as Judaism and Christianity. On the

43

21 Hare Krishna devotees at the opening of their new temple on the island of Inish Rath, County Fermanagh, Northern Ireland, in 1986. Members of the movement follow the teachings of a sixteenth century guru, Chaitanya. Most of Ireland's small Hindu community of Indian origin were present to celebrate the installation of the statues of Krishna and Radha.

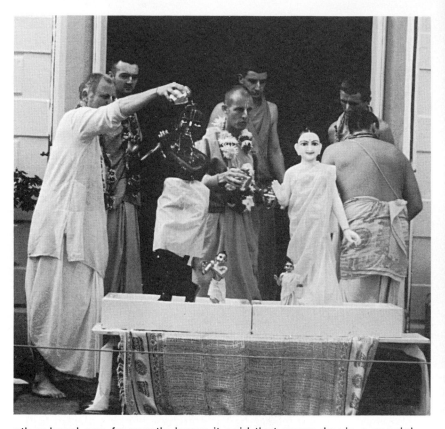

other hand one frequently hears it said that every day is a special holy day for some Hindus somewhere in India. The customary time for devotional acts is early in the morning, immediately after bathing, which many staunch Hindus say should coincide with sunrise. At Mathura, the town sacred to Krishna on the bank of the river Jumna, priests conduct a puja called Jumna Arti while it is dark. It ends at about the time the sun begins to appear. In nearby temples the same Arti ceremony happens a little later. At Banares, pilgrims are to be seen bathing in the river Ganges while it is dark; then as the sun begins to rise across the river they offer their prayers and the devotion of their hearts and minds.

Pilgrims, and people who have the time to devote themselves almost totally to the practice of religion, can be found at temples at any time; most Hindus have a living to earn so during the day they are busy in the fields, in factories, hospitals and offices, or wherever their occupations take them. Temples sometimes close from about 1 o'clock until 4 pm, but in the evening they will open again. As darkness falls so the time for evening devotion arrives. The sounds of the evening Arti ceremony can be heard at about 7 o'clock.

◀

22 Placing a halo round the head of the newly-installed statue of Radha in The Hindu Temple, Southampton, England.

Acts of worship

There are many kinds of acts of worship. We have already noted that many are of an individual nature. It is possible to offer only a flower, but with the sincere heart, and many Hindus give a marigold or a rose as their temple offering. However, the principal act performed by the priests daily morning and evening is Arti, which means the offering of light.

Arti

The priest takes a metal dish with five wick holders or branches, lights these and then begins to wave the dish in front of the statue of the god, or in the case of Jumna Arti towards the river. (At Jumna Arti a huge lamp is used whose flames reach nearly a metre into the sky. It takes a strong priest to lift it.)

The offering of light through the fire is accompanied by the hymn (see opposite page) which all worshippers are encouraged to sing. In Sanskrit it begins with the words 'Om jay jagdish hare, swami jay jagdish hare'.

Havan

Arti is quite simple. The Havan ceremony is extremely elaborate and complex. It takes an hour to perform. The central feature is the sacred fire. The fire, Agni, the purifier and divine messenger, carries the prayers and offerings of the worshippers to heaven. The fire is made in a havan kund, a square clay or metal box with an open top. First, the gifts are brought and consecrated. They consist of flowers, ghee (liquified butter), grain, wood for the fire and a coconut. When a series of prayers has been said, the priest directs worshippers sitting nearest the havan kund to place sticks in the container. Camphor is put in with them so that they will ignite easily. Once the fire is started, grain, ghee and more sticks are added to build it up into quite a fierce blaze. All the while the priest recites or reads sacred Sanskrit texts. As the service proceeds, all the worshippers throw grains of rice or corn into the fire as symbols of their own participation and self-giving. At last the coconut is added. When all the prayers have been said, and before the fire dies down, the Arti ceremony is performed. Apart from the priest many people, women as well as men, take their turn in holding the Arti lamp, while everyone sings the hymn 'Om jay jagdish hare'.

There must be thousands of hymns which Hindus sing, either by themselves as they offer their own individual worship or in groups. One of the best known and most popular is one which simply consists of repeating the names of God. It runs, 'Hare Krishna, Hare Krishna, Krishna, Krishna, Hare, Hare, Hare Rama, Hare

Hindu priest performing Arti.

Rama, Rama, Rama, Hare, Hare', repeated time and time again. Although it is so simple many Hindus would say that it is more powerful and important than any other hymn, for it is calling upon God by name and calling his names to mind. By so doing one takes God into one's heart and becomes God-filled.

TASKS TASKS TASKS TASKS TASKS TASKS

1 Here is an English version of a hymn to Shiva. When you have read it, try to find out as much as you can about the myths and appearance of the god to which it refers.

Hymn to Shiva (in Gujarati)

(References to iconographic/mythological attributes)

1 Om Jayakailasa pati (Repeat)	He whose abode is Mt Kailasa
2 Krupakarine arupo	Please grant us a blessed mind/thought
3 Saune sūbhamati	
Mastabani jangamala	The one who wanders carefree
Kaiyama vicharata: prabhu kaiyama . . .	
Manavadanavadevo.	To your feet come men, demons, gods.
Tamacharane tarata om jaya . . .	
Mukhuta chatano sundare	You will wear a beautiful crown of hair
Siragangadhara prabhu śira . . .	You who catch the Ganges in your hair.
Vyaghrambarana vastr̀o	Whose dress is the tiger-skin
Bhave sajanara om jaya . . .	Who wears it with love.
Phanidharana śanagar	The embellishment of the serpent
Handiparaswari prabhu nandi . . .	Rider upon Nandi (the bull)
Visapachavana hara	You who digest poison
Jayayara tripurari om jaya	Victory to you, the enemy of Tripuri
Ramabhakta tayi preme	Lovingly, Ram becomes your bhakta
Kayamagana kare prabhu kaya . . .	One who sings eternally
Punita charano seve	Punit (a personal name) served at your holy feet.
Te bhavo pārakare om jaya . . .	The one who takes us across the ocean of samsara.

(lines 1, 2, 3 repeated)

---

2 What are the five senses? In Hindu worship all five are used. How?

3 What reasons can you think of which a Hindu might give for starting the day with a bath and puja, which is the name often used for worship?

4 What advantages and disadvantages might there be in using statues or pictures to represent God? Is anything gained or lost by only using names?

5 Discover what you can about some of the other Hindu deities. Collect pictures of them.

6
Thinking about Hinduism

The devotee in any religion may be a person who sincerely performs rituals, keeps festivals, worships and says prayers, but never thinks much about the nature of belief. Religion is something to be lived. God is to be worshipped, depended upon and loved. Not for this worshipper the speculations of theology. At the other extreme is the person who spends his or her life thinking about religion, talking about it, debating it. Among Hindus, both these kinds of religious person can be found, as well as many in between.

One Hindu put it this way. There are five elements, according to Indian thinking: earth, water, air, fire and sky. Everything comes from these. People's attitudes to the gods are just like these elements. There are those who are like the earth. They need something solid to get hold of when they worship. They begin by thinking that the statue is God. As they mature in their faith they recognise that God is like water, formless. Perhaps God can be seen in a statue, but he certainly cannot be given form. Then there are the people who come to think that God is like the air; he has no shape and cannot be seen, only felt. Others will say he is like fire; he can be seen and felt, but not touched or given shape. Others will say he is like the sky; we may think we can see him but he is beyond our control and explanation. As believers pass through these stages they may grow in faith and understanding, yet they will become less certain of what they say. The unsophisticated, those of the way of the earth, are one hundred per cent certain; those of the water eighty per cent; those of fire sixty per cent; those of air forty per cent; and those of sky only twenty per cent sure that they can say anything about God.

Hindu philosophers

For centuries Hindu philosophers have wrestled with questions about the nature of God and the relationship of the world, and especially humanity, to God. They do it not for pleasure and enjoyment, though Hindu philosophy can be fun. They do it so that by understanding the relationship of themselves to God they can achieve liberation, spiritual freedom from the endless cycle of birth, death and rebirth. Hindu philosophy is traditionally about God; it has a definite purpose.

Shankara

This is the name of a philosopher who lived in the eighth century CE. He was a devotee of Shiva, composed hymns to the god and founded a number of monasteries. From his reading of the scriptures he concluded that Brahman, the Sanskrit term for God, is the only eternal reality. All else is illusion in the sense that it has no permanent existence of its own. Thus the gods do not exist, you and I do not exist; either as we think carefully about them they will pass away or at death they will be no more. If Brahman is the only lasting reality, the aim of life must be union with Brahman. Shankara taught that once a person has perceived that Brahman is the only reality, union can be brought about through thought, meditation and contemplation. True knowledge will enable a person to recognise that in a sense he or she is Brahman. With this intuitive knowledge, distinctions of wealth, caste, sex, suffering and all worldly cares and joys will cease to be important.

Ramanuja

Ramanuja lived about two centuries after Shankara. Tradition says he was 120 years old when he died in 1137 or 1157 CE. He did not agree with Shankara's analysis of reality. For him the world is real – to some extent. However, it owes its existence to Brahman who created and sustained it. The universe is dependent on God. It derives its reality from God. God wishes to unite humanity with him; this he does by grace, undeserved and unearned love. For Ramanuja, then, spiritual liberation is achieved through loving devotion, or bhakti. God inspires the worshipper to love him. The love is demonstrated and strengthened by hymn singing, temple worship, home devotion and pilgrimages. For Ramanuja the form which most fully represents God, or Brahman, is Vishnu.

▲
23 A Hindu guru with disciples at the holy city of Hardwar.

Gurus

Although Shankara and Ramanuja are probably the best-known Hindu philosophers, there are many others, all with their teachings and their favoured techniques for achieving God-realisation and freedom from rebirth. Those to whom most Hindus turn today are men, and a few women, called gurus.

Gurus are teachers who can help those who trust them to achieve spiritual liberation because they have already done so themselves. They can take others along the path they have successfully trodden. There is a very famous and ancient Hindu prayer which says,

From the unreal lead me to the real,
From the darkness lead me to light,
From death lead me to immortality.

That is what a guru is believed to do. The guru helps the disciple to see the world as it really is, to cross over from illusion to reality, and in so doing to overcome death and rebirth in becoming immortal.

In the old days sons of the twice-born varnas went to stay with their guru after the initiation ceremony. Now they only make a token gesture. However, there are many Hindus who go in sincerity to gurus and not all the gurus or all the disciples are twice born. Long ago someone who wished to become a disciple would take a bundle of sticks in his hand, approach and offer them to the guru.

◀

24 A brahmin wearing the sacred thread. He protects himself from the sun as he studies one of the scriptures of Hinduism.

If this symbolic gift was accepted, the person who had made it became a disciple. The words used by Hindus for disciple are chela or sishya. Today a fire ceremony may still be used as a way of receiving the initiate. The disciple receives three important things from the guru, besides inner peace and the hope or promise of immortality. One is darshan, virtue or grace which the guru bestows simply through a look. The second is sadhana, spiritual discipline. The guru, like an athletics coach or teacher, sums up the needs of the pupil and provides spiritual exercises which will enable him to master his body, mind and spirit. This may include diet – becoming a vegetarian (perhaps not even eating eggs), study of religious books and the performance of certain tasks. If the guru sees that his disciple is full of self-importance he may give him a menial job to do, such as polishing the shoes of visitors who will have taken off their footwear before coming into the guru's presence. Through darshan and sadhana the disciple receives power, shaktipat. Sometimes this takes the form of being able to undertake unusual feats of endurance – for example, going without food and drink for many days, or being buried alive for a week and emerging unharmed – or it may be the power to experience the union with ultimate reality which the guru himself has had.

The guru is almost a substitute father. Those men and women who go to live with him permanently in a community are often people who have found family life unsatisfactory. Through the guru they discover security, purpose and happiness.

Some gurus form communities which are withdrawn from the world. Such a centre, called an ashram, is a place of retreat. There are, however, gurus who have a strong social conscience, who use the money which they receive from their chelas to build schools and hospitals, speak out against caste discrimination, and encourage village development projects. Their disciples go to the guru for advice and to recharge their spiritual batteries, then they return to the social tasks which he has given them to do. These contributions to the development of Indian society are important but it must be remembered that the reasons for going to the guru are, in the last resort, spiritual. He is not a trainer of social workers and the main aim of his chelas is immortality.

Kabir, a guru who lived five hundred years ago, said,

The pearl is found in the oyster, the oyster is in the sea, the diver brings it up, no one else has the power to do this.

No else has the power to lead from darkness to light, from death to immortality, but many have the power to improve villages.

Karma, samsara, moksha

Hinduism teaches that the soul is eternal and that the soul which has not achieved liberation in this life will be born again and again until that detachment from the material world and the body is realised. It is said that there are 8 400 000, or as Hindus say 84 lakhs, rebirths. Whether this means that the soul could go through all these before being liberated or whether it means that there are that many forms of life which are subject to rebirth, is a matter of debate among Hindus. However, the main thing is not to argue but to avoid being reborn. This is where the guru, the philosophers, the temple, or pilgrimage come in.

Rebirth is the result of karma. This word means action and also the effect of action. The law of karma, as it is often called, is that our deeds result in our being what we are. How we behaved in our last life determines our present birth. What we do now is at this very moment helping to decide what we shall become when we are born next time. The whole process of passing from one body to another – the Sanskrit term for it is samsara, which means wandering – has improvement, perfection and freedom from rebirth as its aim. The purpose of samsara is not punishment but refinement. It is rather like someone trying to extract pure metal from an ore; it may take a number of attempts, with the metal going back into the smelter several times. Ultimately, the metal will emerge pure.

A humorous story is sometimes told to illustrate the process. It is difficult to avoid the conclusion that it was told by a non-brahmin to try to put the brahmins in their place. After all, they sometimes think that theirs is the most superior of all births, a just reward for living virtuously in the previous life; and will be followed almost inevitably by liberation, moksha. Well . . . once upon a time there was a greedy, miserly brahmin, a lover of gold. He performed marriages and other ceremonies not for the welfare of the community but merely to make money. He would take it at night and hide it in a pot in the bank of a river. In this way he managed to hoard a small fortune before he died. When at last he did die he did not attain moksha. Clearly he was not ready for that; his mind was too set on the material things of life. Instead he was born a water rat. Thus he could be near his heart's desire – but he could also learn the lesson that gold is of very limited value. As a water rat, the hoard of gold was worthless to him.

It is not known what happened to the rat in its next life. The point of the story is to warn those who hear it to mend their ways while

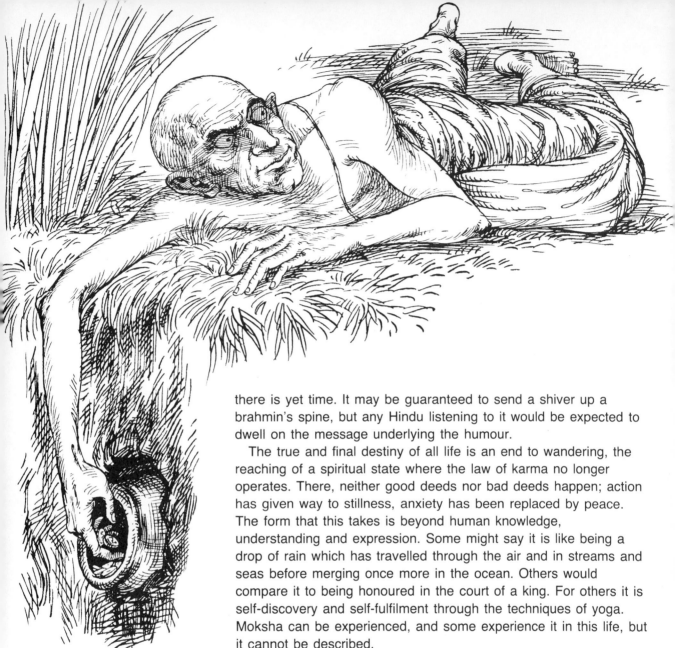

there is yet time. It may be guaranteed to send a shiver up a brahmin's spine, but any Hindu listening to it would be expected to dwell on the message underlying the humour.

The true and final destiny of all life is an end to wandering, the reaching of a spiritual state where the law of karma no longer operates. There, neither good deeds nor bad deeds happen; action has given way to stillness, anxiety has been replaced by peace. The form that this takes is beyond human knowledge, understanding and expression. Some might say it is like being a drop of rain which has travelled through the air and in streams and seas before merging once more in the ocean. Others would compare it to being honoured in the court of a king. For others it is self-discovery and self-fulfilment through the techniques of yoga. Moksha can be experienced, and some experience it in this life, but it cannot be described.

TASKS TASKS TASKS TASKS TASKS TASKS

1 How might the doctrine of karma help a Hindu to understand the inequalities of life? How might the following people explain their situation, using the idea of karma? A poor man, a brahmin, a rich woman, a person born blind.

2 Theologians try to explain difficult concepts such as God, the soul, heaven, or hell. You might begin with something simpler. Explain to your classmates, love, ugliness, beauty, evil, or goodness.

7

The Hindu scriptures

The sacred writings of Hinduism have been compiled over many centuries. They begin with the oldest scriptures in the world, but it is not easy to say where and when they end. There is a sense in which the scriptures are still being revealed – in the teachings of living gurus. There are two groups of scriptures, sruti and smrti. Sruti are those which have been revealed by God directly, to wise men called rishis. Smrti means 'remembered' and this second category of scriptures are remembered sayings. These are considered to have come only indirectly from God, therefore they are less reliable. After all, the human memory is fallible.

The *Veda* is the first of the revealed scriptures. It is divided into four collections or separate books. First there is the *Rig Veda*, a collection of 1028 hymns written in an early form of Sanskrit. These were used in the religious rituals of the Aryan settlers in India nearly four thousand years ago. Secondly came the *Sama Veda*, a rearrangement of some of those hymns, and thirdly the *Yajur Veda*, the verses used by the priests. Fourth came the *Artharva Veda*. This book contains material which is probably not Aryan at all but belonged to the people who were living in northern India when the Aryans invaded and settled the land.

Veda means knowledge. There is another group of books which also belong to this body of knowledge. They are called the *upanishads*. An upanishad is really the collected teachings of a guru. It is often difficult to understand because, of course, the knowledge was meant to be secret, something given by the guru to the disciple, the chela, not to the public at large. There are about thirteen of these major upanishads, written over two and a half thousand years ago, though others of a later date exist and in theory there is nothing to stop anyone writing one today.

The great philosophers such as Shankara and Ramanuja, and many gurus, have based their teachings upon vedanta – a name

▲
25 A meeting for discussion and prayer in The Hindu Temple, Leeds.

which covers both the *Veda* and the *upanishads* – but there are other sacred books which belong to the group called smrti and which have also been important. One of these is the *Manu Smrti*, the so called *Laws of Manu*. Among other things these laid down the code of conduct for the different varnas of Hindu society. Even today the Hindu way of life is greatly influenced by this collection.

Far more popular, however, are the two great epic poems, the *Mahabharata* and the *Ramayana*. The *Mahabharata* was written about 900 BCE. Its title means the Great Epic of the Bharatas. It is 200 000 verses long, the world's longest poem. It is the story of a power struggle between two royal families, the Pandavas and the Kauravas, both descended from King Bharata. The story begins with King Pandu, eldest son of King Bharata, retiring to the forest to live as a sannyasin and leaving his throne to his brother, Dhritarashtra. Naturally, Dhritarashtra took his nephews, the sons of Pandu, into his household and treated them as his own sons. Equally naturally, his sons became jealous of their cousins and decided to murder them by setting fire to the house in which they were living. The five Pandavas heard of the plot in time to escape to the forest. There they lived for a number of years. One of them, Arjuna, eventually emerged, though in disguise. He won an archery contest and with it the hand of a princess called Draupadi. To win the contest not only had he to hit the revolving target in the shape of a fish, he had also to succeed in lifting the greatest bow ever made and drawing its string. The sons of Dhritarashtra knew that there was only one man who possessed enough strength and that man was Arjuna. Fearing that the Pandava princes would exact revenge, the Kauravas agreed to share the kingdom with them, being careful to give them the poorest land. However, as a result of considerable effort these areas became the richest in the kingdom. Angry and fearful, the Kauravas once again planned to rid themselves of their cousins. They persuaded Yudhishthira, the eldest of the Pandavas, to play a game of dice and to gamble with his family's lands as the stake.

Of course, he lost, the land was forfeited and the brothers and Draupadi went into exile. If they could remain unrecognised for thirteen years, they were to be allowed to return and receive back their lands. Needless to say, however, when they had succeeded in satisfying this condition, the Kauravas refused to keep their side of the bargain and instead resorted to war. The Pandavas won. For many years they ruled the kingdom righteously. The story ends with their retirement from the life of action, their dharma fulfilled, to the mountains of the Himalayas to await eternal bliss. This is the brief outline of a story which winds and twists like a river which has reached the plains. It is full of moral and social teaching.

Arjuna winning the contest and with it the princess Draupadi.

The *Ramayana*, being a mere 24 000 Sanskrit verses long, is a short story compared with the *Mahabharata*. Said to have been written by one man, Valmiki, in the fourth century BCE, it too is a moral tale. Rama, the hero, king of Ayodhya, loses his throne and is compelled to go into exile, accompanied by his loyal brother Lakshman and his faithful wife Sita. While Rama is away hunting, Sita is abducted by the evil demon Ravana and taken to his island kingdom of Lanka. With the help of the monkey king, Hanuman, and his army, Sita is found and rescued. Rama returns with her in triumph to his capital city. This story of womanly virtue and the victory of good over evil is one of the most popular in India. It is re-enacted at festivals and on many other occasions throughout the year.

The Bhagavad Gita

People ouside India probably know this Hindu scripture better than any of the others. Its beautiful message of God's love for humanity regardless of sex, caste or creed has won the hearts and minds of many readers. It is included in the sixth book of the *Mahabharata* though it was probably written much later, in about the third century BCE.

The story is of Arjuna preparing to fight his cousins in the terrible war. As the armies line up for battle at a place called Kurukshetra he is struck with horror at the prospect of the slaughter, and especially at the thought of killing kith and kin. It is his Kaurava cousins he is about to fight and although they have wronged the Pandavas he regards what he is about to do as evil. When Arjuna orders his chariot driver to withdraw, he finds himself being given instead a lecture on duty. It turns out that the driver is none other than the god Krishna in human form. Krishna says that because of God's love for him and his love of God, whoever dies in battle will live eternally and whoever lives will achieve the same good through worshipping God. As the story proceeds it becomes clear that it is not about warfare and pacifism but about bhakti, the religion of loving devotion. The *Bhagavad Gita* may have been written at approximately the time when the Laws of Manu were being codified. These represented the view that the shudras and untouchables had no hope of achieving spiritual liberation in their present lives; they must return as 'twice born' in a later existence. The author of the *Gita* rejects this view and maintains that anyone, including women, who worships God with love will go to God; but dharma (the way of life appropriate to one's caste and family) is not to be neglected.

The *Bhagavad Gita* is the first book of what has become known as the bhakti tradition of Hinduism. This has become the popular religion of most Hindus, especially those of the lower castes. Thousands of hymns inspired by the same theme of love, God's love for humanity, and the human response of love have been written over the centuries and continue to be composed. In this sense it may be said that the smrti form of scripture is still alive, with new pieces being produced today.

TASKS TASKS TASKS TASKS TASKS TASKS

1 A modern bhakti hymn called 'My Sweet Lord' was written by one of the Beatles, George Harrison. Try to find a recording of it to play in class. Listen carefully to the words. Write them down if you can and study their meaning. What impression of God do they convey? You might able to do some research and discover how George Harrison came to write the song.

2 Look for some other examples of bhakti hymns. Can you think of any Christian hymns that come into the category of bhakti?

3 Collect some verses from Hindu scriptures and work out what they mean. (For example, see *A Book of World Religions* by E. G. Parrinder pp 108–111 [Hulton].)

8
Festivals and pilgrimages

Every day, it seems, is someone's festival in India. This is not only because every major religion of the world is to be found in that great land but because Hinduism itself has so many. In this book there is only space to mention a few of the better-known ones which are celebrated throughout the country. Even these are enjoyed for different reasons and in a variety of ways depending on the region. One thing is certain, the festivals are enjoyed. Hinduism is a religion that believes that fun and happiness are important, even though religion is a serious matter. Rejoicing and celebration have their place, a place that is there for all to see at festival times. However, this does not mean that a festival is a universal holiday from work. That would be impossible when so many people live in villages. The land has to be irrigated daily, the cows have to be milked and they and other animals have to be fed. Besides, many Indians cannot afford to take a day off work, especially those who are paid by the piece. The farmer will agree a wage for harvesting the rice crop in a particular field; the Banares silk merchant will pay so much for a piece of cloth. A day off work means no money. Only teachers, university, bank and office workers and some other government employees receive holidays with pay. Consequently, early morning is the time at festivals when extra prayers are said or visits made to the temple; evening is when food is enjoyed late into the night. The rule, Indians say, is eat it and beat it. The meal ends the celebration. As soon as it is finished, everyone goes home or to bed.

There are three main Hindu calendars. All of these are lunar so, although new year may vary from region to region, the months begin and end at the same time and have roughly the same name with slight regional variations. Lunar months are divided into two parts: the light half, approaching the full moon, is known as shuklapaksha; and the half related to the waning moon is called krishnapaksha. Krishna means dark.

▶ **26** Indian women carrying flowers at a festival procession in London.

Table of Hindu months and major festivals

Month	Gregorian month	Festival
Chaitra	March/April	**Ugadi** (first day)
Vaisakha	April/May	**Ram Navami**
Jyestha	May/June	
Ashadha	June/July	
Sravana	July/August	**Raksha Bandan**
		Krishna Janamashtami
Bhrapada	August/September	
Asvina	September/October	**Navratri**
		Dussehra
		Diwali
Karttika	October/November	Diwali ends
Margashrsha	November/December	
Pausa	December/January	
Magha	January/February	**Mahashivaratri**
Phalguna	February/March	**Holi**

Ugadi

The new moon of the new year is a time for making a new start. The family will probably rise earlier than usual to sweep the house and the courtyard outside. Following the morning bath, the body is rubbed with sweet scented oils and those who can afford to will put on new clothes. The doorway of the house will be decorated with rangoli patterns – designs made of flour, drawn on the ground. It is a time when many Hindus consult astrologers to discover what the year ahead has in store for them and when members of the twice-born castes will renew the sacred thread.

Ram Navami

The birthday of Lord Rama is accompanied by special pujas and fasting from everyday vegetables, cereals and salt. Instead more unusual delicacies are enjoyed.

Raksha Bandan

Long ago, it is said, the wife of the god Indra saved him from the attack of a demon called Bali by tying a thread round his right wrist.

Now on this day girls tie similar threads, or more elaborate tinsel bracelets, round the wrists of their brothers. These are to claim their protection and to give them protection. The lucky persons who have been chosen are expected to give the girls presents.

Krishna Janamashtami

This is the birthday of the Lord Krishna. Because he was born at midnight, many Hindus stay up all night to keep a vigil. Often a cot is placed in the temple and people come with their small gifts for the infant. Sweets are shared among the children, stories of Krishna are told and there is singing and dancing.

Navratri

Durga, the great female goddess, is worshipped during this festival of nine nights. People fast, taking only one meal a day consisting of fruit and sweetmeats made from milk. The evenings are often spent dancing. The main story associated with Navratri is that of Rama and Sita from the *Ramayana* of Valmiki. In this narrative Rama had to turn to Durga for help in overthrowing Ravana.

Long ago this was probably a harvest festival. One of the features of the dances is the use of sticks to make actions which resemble those of harvesters cutting corn with sickles.

▼

27 Preparing for the Dussehra celebrations in New Delhi at which the firework-filled statues of Ravana, flanked by his two brothers, will be set on fire.

Dussehra

This festival falls on the tenth day, the day after Navratri. On this day the statue of Durga, which villagers have been using as an aid to worship during the earlier festival, is taken to the river and placed in the water. The procession to the river is very joyful and the villagers sing and clap as the image sinks below the water for they believe that with it, symbolically, goes all unhappiness and misfortune. This is also Vijaya Dashami, the Glorious Tenth, when Rama, Lakshman and Hanuman rescued Queen Sita from Ravana's clutches. The theme of friendship as well as fidelity and courage runs through the *Ramayana*. This is a time for ending quarrels, holding theatrical performances to tell the story of Rama and Sita and burning Ravana in effigy and firework displays.

Diwali

This is the best-known festival of all. It lasts for five days, beginning at the dark end of one month and extending into the new moon days of the next. The name means cluster of lights and refers to the rows of clay lamps which are to be found outside every home and temple and inside many houses.

The fight against Ravana is now completely over and Rama and Sita return to Ayodhya where their joyful subjects greet them with lights. The darkness of evil has been dispelled. The good times have come back. All these ideas are present in the celebration of Diwali. This festival also marks another Hindu new year. There is special house cleaning, rangoli patterns are made and presents, especially new clothes, are given. Even the cattle will probably be given a good scrub as one of the acts of preparation and the walls of the cow shed may be newly whitewashed. Vishnu's defeat of the demon Bali, the one from whom Indra had to be protected, is also a reason for celebrating Diwali. The story of that exploit will be told to children during the festival. The goddess Lakshmi is reputed to visit the homes of good children, bringing gifts to them and prosperity to their family.

Mahashivaratri

This winter festival is sacred to Shiva. It is the anniversary of his marriage to the goddess Parvati and the time when his devotees remember him saving humanity by drinking a draught of poison with which a demon was planning to kill the population of the world. The day is a fast until late afternoon when a special puja is offered to Shiva. Then the fast is broken with sweet potatoes and cucumber, but no cereals or curries may be eaten. Unmarried women should fast and keep a vigil throughout the night in the hope that Shiva will find them husbands. The next day is a feast day for everyone.

Holi

This is the most colourful festival. It is also an occasion for licensed mischief-making. Children take water coloured with dye and either throw it or squirt it from cycle pumps at passers-by. No respect is paid to anyone on grounds of age or status.

Long ago a king by the name of Hiranyakapishu proclaimed himself to be a god and ordered everyone to worship him and no one else. His young son Prahlad refused. The king asked his daughter, who possessed great powers, to get rid of the boy. One of her powers was that of being able to walk through fire, but she did not realise that this was only effective when she entered the fire alone. When she carried Prahlad into the flames, it was she who perished; he came out alive because he had kept on repeating the names of God, 'Hare Krishna'. With this story in mind, mothers carry their babies round village bonfires, in a clockwise direction of course, praying that God will protect them from harm.

Pilgrimage

The apparently endless round of festivals (to which Christmas could be added, because Hindus do not only celebrate their own special days) is accompanied by what is certainly an endless round of pilgrimages. The people of India seem to be continually on the move: the streets seem never to go silent or become empty. Much of this movement is directed towards places of pilgrimage.

According to some Hindus, there are 64 000 places of pilgrimage, but this is just a round figure to indicate that the numbers are countless. Wherever earth and sky, land and water, or two rivers meet, there is somewhere that is especially holy. To it pilgrims will come. There are towns like Hardwar at the head of the Ganges, Banares (the sacred city of Shiva) and Vrindaban, the birthplace of Krishna. They owe their present existence and prosperity, if not their origins, to their importance as pilgrimage centres.

Let us take one of them, Vrindaban, as an example. The visitor arriving at Mathura station can take a bus or go by tonga, or walk of course. If the visitor goes by tonga, he or she will have the driver – his voice competing with the horse's hooves – telling him about the places they are passing. Here the youthful Krishna danced all night with the cowgirls; there, as a naughty child, he upset his mother's churn of milk. Somewhere else while his mother's back was turned, he stole the butter which she had made. Without much effort it is possible to imagine those long-ago events and hear the sound of Krishna's flute carried through the trees by the breeze. On the road to Vrindaban it is possible to believe that this is no ordinary journey. Once there the pilgrim goes from temple to temple, some old, some very new, expressing his devotion to Krishna.

Who goes on pilgrimage? The answer is anyone or everyone. It may be a large family group, including grandmother but with grandfather conspicuous by his absence. He has recently died; the pilgrimage is to place his ashes in the river Ganges at Banares, and to pray for the wellbeing of his soul. Or it may be a newly married couple, or a brother and sister whose parents are now too old and infirm to undertake the pilgrimage themselves. Sometimes almost an entire village will take itself off to a nearby place, perhaps twenty miles away, walking the whole distance. They may go because of an annual festival, or because of an eclipse, or because they have heard that a well-known guru is going to attend the place and they wish to receive darshan.

TASKS TASKS TASKS TASKS TASKS TASKS

1 Organise an assembly or party (or both) to celebrate a Hindu festival. You will need to:
   a tell the story of the festival and explain its meaning or meanings;
   b describe how the festival would be celebrated by Hindus.
   You might be able to learn some dances or songs. You might be able to cook some Indian foods or at least buy sweets.

2 After studying festivals in some other religions, discuss the importance of festivals in religions.

3 What non-religious occasions do we celebrate? Why?

9
Hinduism in Britain

There are about 350 000 Hindus in Britain. It is not easy to provide accurate statistics because the censuses this century have not asked people to state their religious beliefs.

Most of Britain's Hindus have come from India of course, usually from the west coast, especially the state of Gujarat, or from Punjab in the north west. Others have come from East Africa where they had settled in such countries as Kenya, Uganda or Tanzania. These are themselves descendants of Gujarati or Punjabi Indians. You may also come across Hindus from the island of Mauritius and some from Trinidad or Guyana in the Caribbean. It is usual to think

▼
28 Alvin Kallicharan, former captain of the West Indies cricket team, is of Indian origin.

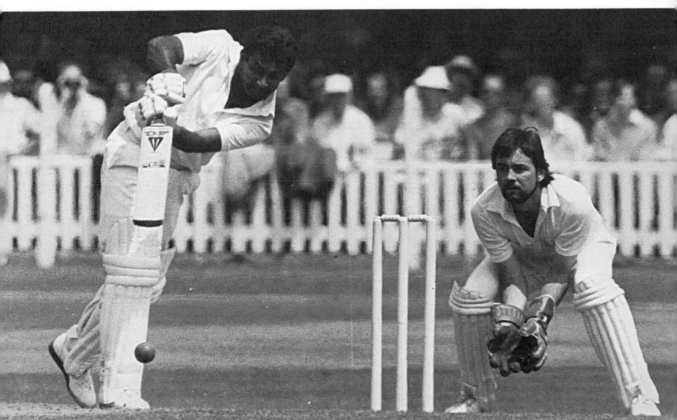

of West Indians as people of African origin but when the slave trade was stopped and slavery came to an end, in the nineteenth century, a number of Chinese as well as Indians emigrated to British territories in the Caribbean to work as labourers on the plantations. Some of the Indians were Muslim but most were Hindus. One Caribbean Hindu, Alvin Kallicharan, captained the West Indian test cricket team in the 1970s.

The majority of Hindus who came to Britain arrived in the 1950s though a few came much earlier, even before the First World War, and many wives and families came later. Nowadays, except for some voucher holders from East Africa, there are no Hindus entering Britain. Immigration from India and the Caribbean has been stopped. Indian Hindus came to Britain in search of work. There were few opportunities in their own country so they turned to the place they had been taught to call their motherland, Britain, which was advertising in many parts of the Commonwealth for people to work in its factories, hospitals and transport services. East African Hindus also came in search of work, but they left Africa where they had been very successful and prosperous because of the policy of Africanisation which was introduced once the British left. The governments of Kenya, Uganda and Tanzania encouraged Africans to fill government posts and senior appointments in industry. Many Indians, who were British citizens and had never even visited India, decided to use their British passports and answer Britain's call for workers.

Hindus settled in most of Britain's major industrial cities, especially London, Leicester, Coventry, Birmingham, Bristol, Leeds, Southampton and Manchester. They have now dispersed to many other areas. They have also set up small businesses and shops, or become teachers, doctors, insurance agents, computer operators, though many are to be found in textile mills, factories, or in transport, where they first found employment. Hindus can settle anywhere. They do not need to attend the temple, they do not even need special shops as many supermarkets now sell the foodstuffs Indians require because large numbers of Britons are now using ingredients of Indian cookery. It is at festival times such as Navratri or Diwali that Hindus especially like to get together. Then they will make long journeys to one of the thirty-nine or so temples in the United Kingdom. We say 'long journeys' but for Hindus from Africa or India, used to travelling for three or four days non-stop, a drive from Land's End to John O'Groats would not seem far. In practice probably no Hindu is more than a two-hour car ride from the nearest temple – not far to go on a Sunday to celebrate a festival and meet friends and relatives.

Hindu life in Britain differs from life in India in a number of ways. Caste matters far less. Everyone is accepted in the temples and at family gatherings. The most caste-conscious Hindus would never cross the Kali Pani (the Black Ocean), as they call the sea, to become permanently polluted in a non-Hindu land. Caste still matters in marriage – most weddings are arranged on caste lines – but Hindus in Britain are more likely to experience colour or race discrimination from other people, than caste discrimination from Hindus, if they experience any hostilities at all.

The temple is where the biggest change is to be noticed. In India there will be over thirty in a small town, some of them only wayside shrines. In England at present there are only thirty-nine, of which seventeen have been purpose-built. The rest are buildings which were bought by Hindus and converted into temples. The temple in Britain has become a place for congregational worship where services are held at weekends and on some mornings and evenings. It is also a community centre where children learn to read and write their parents' mother tongue, Hindi, Gujarati or Punjabi; here they also learn Indian dancing and perhaps Hinduism. The things which came naturally to a child in a Hindu community in India now have to be taught in temple schools.

The temple is also a community centre for adults. Once the women gossiped daily at the village well, the men gathered under

▲
29 Arti at a Hindu temple, Leeds.

▲
30 Women singing hymns in a Hindu temple at Southall, London.

the verandah of a house after the day's work was done. Now the temple is the meeting place, perhaps once a week or less frequently. It is also the place where Hindus can share community problems and maybe arrange marriages.

In India much of one's life is lived outdoors. Weddings are held on open ground. Festivals are often open-air events. The village cinema, as has been mentioned, is a travelling show mounted on a lorry, watched in the warm night air. In Britain Hinduism has to take shelter indoors. Even in the summer the weather is unpredictable, so Hinduism takes to the temple. No longer does it seem to be primarily the home of God; it becomes the home of the community.

Much is done to retain the Indian character of Hinduism. Banyan tree leaves, betel nuts and other necessities may be flown in from India for use at weddings and other celebrations, but often substitutions are made. For example, there is a ceremony called Vadh puja when a family remembers the anniversary of a child's death. In India an offering of rice and milk would be placed at the foot of a vadh tree, chosen because it bears no fruit. In Britain, there are no vadh trees, so here, when the family makes the offering, they place the dish under a tree in their garden.

So life goes on and British Hindus, like all religious migrants, attempt to retain the essentials of their culture accommodating, where necessary, to their new circumstances.

◀ **31** Learning how to put on a sari.

TASKS TASKS TASKS TASKS TASKS TASKS

1 Compare what you have learned about Hindu temples in India with temples in Britain. What are the main differences? How are they to be explained?

2 Imagine you were going to live in another country. What aspects of your culture would you hope to retain? How would you decide what things to keep and what to let go? (For example, consider food, pleasure, clothing.)

3 Discover where your nearest Hindu temple is. Try to arrange a visit. When you get there, try to find out:

　a where its members lived before they came to Britain, when they came and why;

　b where people come from Sunday by Sunday or at festival times;

　c what events take place there besides acts of worship.

4 Take or collect photographs and set up a school exhibition related to the visit to the Hindu temple and to this course. You could entitle your exhibition 'Hindus in India – and in our town'. (Of course you must ask permission first, but usually Hindus are happy for photographs to be taken.)

10 Hinduism today and tomorrow

Hinduism is a dynamic, lively religion. It has changed and it will keep on developing as anything that is healthy does. Long ago, before there was the name Hinduism, the religion of India was confronted by the alien beliefs and practices of the people called the Aryans who invaded the country and settled in it. They brought new gods and new ways of worship. Their religion was based upon sacrifice and conducted by the brahmin priests. They divided society into the four varnas and most of the original inhabitants probably became the shudras or outcastes. They seem to have believed that at the end of one's life, the soul went either to a kind of heaven, the abode of the gods, or to the house of clay, a hell. Yet Hindus now accept the idea of rebirth, temples are accompanied by bathing places and there is the popularity of the

▼
32 Buildings in modern New Dehli combine aspects of eastern and western architecture.

33 Aircraft production is one of the new industries of developing India.

34 Apprentices, whose parents may well have been farm labourers, learning to use modern machinery in a training school at Pune (Poona).

bhakti religion based on Krishna or sometimes Shiva, neither of whom are gods found in the *Veda*. In other words, it looks as though the old religion managed to survive and influence the new. So the *Bhagavad Gita* accepts the notion of caste duty – Arjuna should fight for he is a kshatriya – yet anyone who believes in Krishna will attain spiritual liberation. Another example of fusion is prayers for the ancestors who are in heaven. They need those prayers and offerings to prolong the period there before they are reborn on earth. Heaven and rebirth, ideas from two different traditions can come together.

What will happen to Hinduism in the next century it would be foolish to predict, but it may be possible to suggest a few developments. The most famous Hindu of the twentieth century so far has been Mahatma Gandhi, a great nationalist who did much to help India achieve political independence from Britain. He was also an important religious figure, so greatly revered that some Hindus regarded him as another avatar of Vishnu. It might not be surprising to find temples to the Mahatma being set up, but even more likely is the development of Hinduism upon the lines which he suggested.

Gandhi was very much moved by the teaching of the *Bhagavad Gita*, especially the idea of desireless action, the service of one's fellow humans without any wish for reward or gain of any kind. Sometimes Hinduism has been described as a world-denying religion, one which encourages its members to turn their backs on the world's needs, upon the sufferings of the poor and the privileges of the rich, and withdraw instead to meditate in the forest. Such a picture is misleading. Take the example of Gandhi, for instance: at the age of seventy-nine he was socially and politically active when he was assassinated. Though he was twice born, being a vaishya, there was no fourth stage of sannyasin for him. Many Hindus today see him as the ideal Hindu, their inspiration as they work to create modern India. They may not follow all his ideals, but that of action they accept.

Gandhi's teaching that untouchability is a crime against humanity is one which is now a part of the Indian Constitution; gradually it is also being obeyed in practice. Eventually untouchability may be a memory only. As for the caste system generally, it remains most important where marriage is concerned, but the Hindu's life remains very much determined by birth. It is far better to be born a brahmin than a shudra. Maybe another Gandhi is needed to take up the cause of the chamars and chuhras – and of women. Possibly there will appear a guru whose message will move Hindus to action in these matters, for certainly new gurus will rise up in that land where the experience of religion matters more than doctrine or arguments over which form of religion is true. Some of those gurus will go west, to Europe and America, not only because there are Hindus settled in such countries as Britain and the USA, and not in the hope of becoming rich, but because they are aware that many elements of Hinduism have a worldwide appeal – not the caste system, but meditation, for instance, and the idea of a spiritual teacher, a guru, who can speak to each individual according to his or her particular needs.

TASKS TASKS TASKS TASKS TASKS TASKS

1 From your study of Hinduism how might it change in India in the next generation (e.g. caste, marriage, wealth)?

2 Has your study of Hinduism made you change your thinking about what the word 'religion' means? If so, in what ways?

3 How has studying Hinduism helped you to understand how people
   a differ in what is important to them?
   b make decisions in their lives?
   c accept social conditions?

Index